MIXED-RACE
SUPERMAN

MIXED-RACE SUPERMAN

KEANU, OBAMA, AND MULTIRACIAL EXPERIENCE

WILL HARRIS

MELVILLE HOUSE
BROOKLYN · LONDON

MIXED-RACE SUPERMAN

A different version of this work was published in the UK in 2018 by Peninsula Press
Copyright © Will Harris, 2018, 2019
All rights reserved
First Melville House Printing: July 2019

Melville House Publishing   and   Suite 2000
            46 John Street   16/18 Woodford Road
        Brooklyn, NY 11201   London E7 0HA

mhpbooks.com
@melvillehouse

ISBN: 978-1-61219-789-0
ISBN: 978-1-61219-790-6 (eBook)

Designed by Jo Anne Metsch

Library of Congress Cataloging-in-Publication Data

Names: Harris, Will, author.
Title: Mixed-race Superman : Keanu, Obama, and multiracial experience / Will
*   Harris.*
Description: Brooklyn : Melville House, [2019] | "A different version of this
*   work was published in the UK in 2018 by Peninsula Press." | Includes*
*   bibliographical references.*
Identifiers: LCCN 2019018220 (print) | LCCN 2019020013 (ebook) | ISBN
*   9781612197906 (reflowable) | ISBN 9781612197890 (pbk.)*
Subjects: LCSH: Racially mixed people. | Racially mixed people--Race
*   identity. | Racially mixed families. | Miscegenation.*
Classification: LCC HT1523 (ebook) | LCC HT1523 .H38 2019 (print) | DDC
*   305.8--dc23*
LC record available at https://lccn.loc.gov/2019018220

Printed in the United States of America

10 9 8 7 6 5 4 3 2 1

"This body will take some getting used to . . .
It feels unreal to me. Alien."

—KLAATU (KEANU REEVES),
The Day the Earth Stood Still

MIXED-RACE SUPERMAN

used to say that, in the film of my life, Keanu Reeves would play the starring role. Most people don't realize he's mixed race.

Keanu's father is Hawaiian-Chinese—hence his name, Hawaiian for "cool breeze over the mountains"—but since he passes as white that's how people think of him.

An old friend, Tirzah Lea Tward, is quoted in Sheila Johnston's biography of Keanu as saying that "if you asked him where he came from or what his roots were, he was anything you wanted him to be."[1] I like to think that, not quite white and not wanting to constantly explain his "roots," he was trying to get his friends to see race differently: not as a fixed sign but as a fluid signifier. Like a cool breeze, he turned his shapelessness into a form of resistance.

When I was at school I wanted my roots to be mysterious too, but unlike Keanu I don't pass as white. As soon as a conversation turned toward the Orient—Chinese food in the cafeteria, a new Jet Li movie, the other Chinese kid in our year (who was actually Korean)—I'd get these sidelong glances. Asked where I was from, I'd hide behind my mixedness.

I'm one quarter Dutch; most of my family live in Indonesia; my great-great-grandma was from Hokkien; my granddad was a French teacher; I've lived in London my whole life . . .

Keanu could choose whether or not to wear the cape of whiteness: an accepted outsider, different and the same, he was capable of spanning the contradictions within himself. Though it now seems shameful to admit, his was the sinuous and racially unmarked version of the face that I wanted to present to the world.

Recently, an elderly woman in a café asked where I was from, or where I was really from. "Gosh," she said, "those Chinese genes are powerful."

"I don't think it works like that," I said, and started saying something about genetics and race—how they have almost nothing in common—before trailing off. She wasn't listening. "Have you heard of Keanu Reeves?" I asked.

A mixed-race superhero is a contradiction in terms. A superhero might start out like any other confused child, but that confusion soon gives way. The would-be superhero will be injured, taken prisoner, or exposed to cosmic radiation and, later, after a dark night of the soul, they'll emerge into the bright field of self-knowing.

Their voice will change in pitch and their punches will carry more heft, now having behind them the weight of conviction, of an assured identity. Even with his superpowers, Peter Parker couldn't save his uncle from being killed because he wasn't yet Spider-Man. He didn't *know himself*.

As a child, I was confused. I believed myself to be white. At the barber's, I'd ask for hair like Michael Owen or Peter Parker and nobody said anything. Then one day people started asking me where I was from. How long had I been in the country? Could I speak Chinese? My Western name provoked raised eyebrows. My British accent came as a surprise. I could no longer look in the mirror and believe myself to be white, but what was I?

Had I been a superhero, my confusion might have given way to the discovery of some transcendent new identity. But I remained confused, unable to square my experience with the way the world saw me. If mixed-race superheroes do exist, maybe they're people who have found a way to know themselves in spite of themselves. They've worked out how to make their confusion heroic, to embody contradiction.

onsider that game where you have to describe a thing without saying the word for it. The quickest way is by naming its opposite—*black* if you want someone to think *white*, or *man* for *woman*. Though black isn't the opposite of white nor man the opposite of woman, the mind falls easily into the simplest of patterns: either/or.

In A *Cyborg Manifesto*, Donna Haraway talks about the pervasiveness of certain dualisms in the West: mind/body, culture/nature, active/passive. Whether or not these concepts are opposed, they've been hitched together for so long that they've come to prop up—and to depend on—one another's meaning.

The category of the Other, Simone de Beauvoir suggested, is "as original as consciousness itself."[2]

In other words, we have a habit of defining ourselves by what we're not. For Haraway, the dualism between Self and Other is essential to how we as non-cyborgs think about ourselves: The Self dominates while the Other is dominated; the

Self is active, while the Other is passive; the Self is associated with mind and culture, the Other with nature and the body; the Self is pure and white, the Other black, brown, yellow, or otherwise tainted.

Haraway concludes sadly that "one is too few and two is too many"[3]—no single idea can make sense on its own, but no two ideas can be grasped simultaneously.

The mixed-race person embodies this. With too many heritages or too few, too white or not white enough, the mixed-race person grows up to see the self as something strange and shifting—a shadow on the roadside—shaped around a lack. Whereas most superheroes build their identity around a clearly established sense of Self (buttressed by its opposition to an evil Other), the mixed-race superhero must forge their identity in the confusing space between.

rowing up in West London in the mid-nineties and then through the long New Labour years, I rarely heard anyone talk about race beyond stock phrases to do with "multi-culturalism" and the need for "integration" that sometimes made it onto the *Nine O'Clock News*. And though I may have guessed that it was people like me and my mum they were talking about, I pushed the thought aside out of embarrassment.

Then in 1993, a teenager named Stephen Lawrence was killed while waiting for a bus in Eltham, South London. He was with his friend Duwayne Brooks when a group of five white men ran toward them. "What, what, nigger?" shouted one, while another took out a blade. Duwayne saw a flash of metal and thought it was a steel bar. He started to run and called for his friend to follow, but Stephen was bleeding badly. He ran for just over one hundred yards before collapsing by the side of the road.

Despite tip-offs from local residents and clear evidence pointing to the identities of the suspects—who were previously involved in other knife attacks in the area—the Metropolitan

Police refused to act. Leads weren't followed up on and evidence was lost. Duwayne, traumatized, was treated as a suspect and accused of stealing soft drinks during one visit to the police station.[4]

The police's mishandling of the case brought back memories of the 1980s: of stabbings uninvestigated; the indiscriminate use of stop and search; the shooting of Cherry Groce, paralyzed in front of her eleven-year-old son, which led to the first of the 1985 Brixton riots; the death of Cynthia Jarrett, who suffered heart failure when her home was raided by police. No police officers were held accountable, and no apologies were issued.

Stephen Lawrence's killers were eventually arrested, only to walk free a few months later. Then in 1995, twenty-six-year-old Wayne Douglas died in police custody and riots broke out in Brixton again.

None of this had an obvious impact on me. I remember Stephen Lawrence's face on the news and splashed across front pages, cutting through in a way the murders of other young people of color hadn't—maybe because he was so manifestly bright and innocent. The same smiling photograph of him accompanied most news reports, but in my memory it has no context. My parents, if it came up, would only say *tragic* and shake their heads. They never talked about race. Instead, my dad said I should never trust anyone and my mum told me not to look strangers in the eyes.

I n the midst of this, after almost two decades of Conservative government, Tony Blair appeared. The feel-good politics of Bill Clinton's 1992 campaign—socially progressive but fiscally, as it turned out, conservative—had taken a few years to reach British shores. By 1996, though, "Things Can Only Get Better" was ringing out in conference halls up and down the country.

This was Labour, but not as before. The language of its party constitution, for example, had changed: once committed to nationalization—providing workers with "the full fruits of their industry" and "the most equitable distribution" of wealth— it now talked vaguely of "community" and "respect."

The same fuzziness extended to social issues. Just as Clinton was jokingly referred to as the "first black president,"[5] so Tony Blair sought a more outward-looking, diverse leadership. In May 1997, the week Labour won the election, *The Observer* ran the headline "Goodbye Xenophobia." The last Conservative Prime Minister, John Major, had balked at discussing race, saying that "policy must be color blind,"[6] but the New Labour manifesto boldly claimed "our attitudes to race, sex and sexuality have changed fundamentally."[7]

This seemed to be a turning point: an admission that Britain had failed on race—along with "sex and sexuality"—and that New Labour's policies would work to redress the legacy of empire and its accrued inequalities. Instead of detail, though, there was a caveat: "our task is to combine change and social stability." For Stephen Lawrence's family or for those South London communities living with the threat of racist attacks and police brutality, there was little "social stability" to protect. But this kind of rhetoric gave a clearer idea of what to expect. On the one hand, "change" would be necessary and loudly proclaimed; on the other, Labour would remain the party for those who didn't want—and were even terrified of—"change."

For Blair, like Clinton, the appearance of change and compassion was all-important. He didn't want to risk looking callous, overlooking the needs of ethnic minorities, but neither did he want to appear weak, giving in to the demands of identity-based "pressure groups." So toward the end of his tenure in 2006, Blair could give a speech in praise of "multiculturalism," which also said: "Our tolerance is part of what makes Britain, Britain. So conform to it; or don't come here."[8]

"Multiculturalism" became New Labour's rallying cry. It was a term which offended no one by including everyone. It suggested tolerance, while saying conform or else. Beneath its harmonious veneer lay the threat of violence.

Just as New Labour wanted, I grew up not really thinking about race or thinking it was something to *see past*. But its effects were visible everywhere around me.

At school, the kids who got free meals were black and brown, as were the men being stopped and searched on the high street. Later, when there were insults on the playground and I became insecure about my own foreign-looking features, my response was to see past it all, to wait until things got better.

When New Labour came to power, the pressure was such that they were forced to commission a report into Stephen Lawrence's murder and the failure of the police investigation. After two years and countless interviews, the Macpherson Report was presented to Parliament and stated in no uncertain terms that "institutional racism" had undermined the investigation: it pointed to the family's treatment at the hospital, the initial reaction to Duwayne Brooks, and—which was related—the failure of so many officers "to recognise Stephen's murder as a purely 'racially motivated' crime." As Duwayne told the Guardian in 1999, "At the scene the police treated me like a liar, like a suspect instead of a victim, because I was black and they couldn't believe that white boys would attack us for nothing."[9]

The report also noted that "not a single officer questioned before us in 1998 had received any training of significance in racism awareness and race relations throughout the course of his or her career." This might have explained another factor hampering the murder investigation: "the significant under-reporting of 'racial incidents' occasioned largely by a lack of confidence in the police and their perceived unwillingness to take such incidents seriously."[10]

Tony Blair was undaunted. Accustomed to announcing "new eras" and periods of "national renewal," he said there would be "a new era of race relations." This was only a small setback on the road to multicultural prosperity. In the meantime, Stephen's killers went about their lives and I made sure not to look anyone in the eyes.

In February 2007 in Springfield, Illinois, the same city where Abraham Lincoln had launched his political career, Barack Obama announced his run for the presidency. Temperatures were subzero outside the Old State Capitol and those around him wore thick scarves and gloves. Meanwhile, he exuded a benign, hatless warmth, impervious to the cold (I later read online that a heater had been placed under his podium).

In Lincoln's hometown, Obama quoted the great man's words, calling on "a house divided to stand together."

I recently realized that, in my memory, I had mangled his words to "a house divided against himself cannot stand." I must have preferred that version because that's what it felt like he was saying to me: he wouldn't be divided against himself. In becoming the embodiment of a mixed nation, he would transcend its divisions.

I was a shy eighteen-year-old confused about my identity, and Obama spoke to my desire for "a certain presumptuousness, a certain audacity." My experience of politics had been the grinning managerialism of New Labour. After a decade of waiting for a "new era" to arrive, I wanted a superman: a comic book narrative of self-discovery that would compensate for my own self-ignorance.

Now here was a politician who not only looked different, but talked beautifully—and knowingly—of his mixed-race upbringing. Here was a story that was long and painful but seemed to bend implacably toward justice. As I slouched in my freezing university dorm room, watching him on my laptop, his voice booming through its tinny built-in speakers, maybe I did weep a little. I was living away from home for the first time listening to a man who, unlike me in most ways, had named a problem I'd felt my whole life: I was divided against myself. He invoked "a journey," an "improbable quest," "a future of endless possibility"—phrases which, in hindsight, sound like taglines for a bad fantasy film—that made my confusion seem epic and important. His speech over, he turned toward his wife Michelle, who was wearing a velvet bucket hat and looked happy. Jackie Wilson's "(Your Love Keeps Lifting Me) Higher and Higher" was playing to the crowds.

In David Remnick's biography *The Bridge: The Life and Rise of Barack Obama*, a picture emerges of someone who, even during his years of self-described "adolescent rebellion,"[11] was still, according to Margot Mifflin, a friend from Occidental College, "too sophisticated, too smooth somehow."[12]

According to Lisa Jack, another friend from the time, he was "a hot, nice, everything-going-for-him dude."[13] Everywhere he went, people commented on his looks, his self-composure. When Michelle Robinson first set eyes on him in 1989, Remnick says, he was wearing a sports jacket, a cigarette dangling from his mouth, and her first thought was "Oh, here you go. Here's this good-looking, smooth-talking guy."[14] Obama carried the hero's unconscious air of being *chosen*.

In 1995, though, Obama didn't even make the front cover of his own memoir. When *Dreams from My Father* came out, it featured two black-and-white photographs of the black and white sides of his family, along with a drawing of a rural Kenyan scene. It was a sensitively told story about the author's mixed-race family and his coming of age that sold modestly. It wasn't until the reprint in 2004 that the focus shifted. Obama was a public figure by then, touted as a future president and about to become, at the age of 43, the only black senator in the United States.

Mine is the UK edition of the reprint, which has a large photograph of him on the front cover. Against the roaring sea, he stands, brows furrowed, arms folded, staring into the middle-distance. It's the dynamic, reassuring pose of a superhero, held in check by a tiny stoop of the back which suggests not bad posture—too many hours in the library—but a measure of wariness. He looks to his right, almost behind himself. At his back, time's winged chariot hurries near. He's impatient for the future. Or maybe the photographer just wanted to make his ears look smaller. The effect, anyway, is of hope. The waves of history that roll unnoticed past most of us are stilled in his presence.

"Once did people say God when they looked out upon distant seas," wrote Nietzsche, "now, however, I have taught you to say Superman."[15]

The idea of the superman—as distinct from the hero of Greek myth—is often associated with Nietzsche and, by extension, with the blond-haired Aryan soldiers of Nazi propaganda. But most of the time Nietzsche's *Übermensch* comes across as a mess of contradictions. Entirely selfish at one moment, the next he "gives away and does not want to preserve himself."[16] The *Übermensch* doesn't only celebrate the self; he is someone who overcomes it.

Nietzsche wrote *Thus Spoke Zarathustra* quickly, in a haze of pain as much as inspiration. At the time, his eyesight was failing and his digestive system so weak that his doctor forbade him from drinking coffee or smoking after meals. He held to his personal maxim, *virescit volnere virtus* (power grows through wounds), consoling himself with the thought that those who were weak and wounded could most easily see through the weeds of custom. The superman, for him, was not the strongman. Those already strong stood to benefit most from keeping the established order in place.

It's important to note, though, that *Thus Spoke Zarathustra* was written as poetic prophecy, not as a philosophical tract.

Amid the calls for self-overcoming, it left space for doubt, and in this space darker readings of his work have always festered. The *Übermensch*, for example, is often pictured as a swooping eagle or a lion. "To create freedom for oneself," wrote Nietzsche, "the lion is needed."[17] Fascists would take lines like these and imagine themselves as roaring *Übermenschen*, tearing up decadent European society and remaking it in their image.

"Better to live a day as a lion than 100 years as a sheep," Benito Mussolini is supposed to have said. In February 2016, Donald Trump retweeted this quotation with #MakeAmerica GreatAgain. Asked about whether he felt comfortable retweeting a fascist dictator, he said to NBC's Chuck Todd: "It's OK to know it's Mussolini . . . It's a very good quote, it's a very interesting quote."[18] (As an aside, not that this makes Trump look better, the Mussolini quotation itself was tweeted by a bot set up by an editor at Gawker to bait Trump into retweeting it—its avatar featured a grumpy Mussolini sporting a Trumpian bouffant.)

After Trump's inauguration in January 2017, the alt-right website Breitbart heralded "The Age of the Lion."[19] If you look at one of Breitbart's thousands of invectives against the contemporary world it's clear that the lion's vocabulary, as Nietzsche predicted, is limited to a loud "No." This was why Nietzsche added that the lion needed to transform itself into the child. Whereas the lion can only say "No," the child is "innocence and forgetting . . . a sacred 'Yes.'"[20] The Nietzschean superman is a mixed being, denying and affirming, forceful and passive. But the final form the superman takes should be that of a child, defined not by strength but vulnerability.

In May 1840, the Scottish writer Thomas Carlyle gave a series of lectures in London. Known as "the Sage of Chelsea," he attracted an array of literary figures eager to hear his insights, among them William Makepeace Thackeray, Charles Dickens, John Stuart Mill, and Harriet Martineau. According to Julian Symons, his biographer, "the success of the lectures was due in part to the nervousness of the lecturer, the battle he so plainly fought to ejaculate the thoughts within him."[21] Carlyle used a different bodily image in a letter to his mother, describing how he'd shivered through one lecture, vomiting forth words "like wild Annandale grapeshot."[22]

Whatever the eccentricities of his public persona, Carlyle had latched onto a latent mood. Great Men wanted to hear about other Great Men and, more than that, they wanted to believe in a vision of the whole of history as "at bottom the History of Great Men."[23] Where the past was dark and chaotic, he showed it to them illuminated by pinpricks of light—Odin and Muhammed some way off, with Luther and Rousseau closer by. Carlyle was their guide, able to navigate the stars. Later,

Nietzsche would read and take inspiration from the published version—all six lectures bound together and released under the title *On Heroes, Hero-Worship, and The Heroic in History*.

Turning his lectern into a pulpit, Carlyle denounced those who had reduced "this God's-world to a dead brute Steam-engine."[24] Where was the wonder in a steam engine? It made active humans into passive cargo; it sapped the will. History, for him, was "the past, the present, and the future; what was done, what is doing, what will be done; the infinite conjugation of the verb *To do*."[25]

Carlyle blamed the popularity of utilitarianism for much of what was wrong with Victorian society. Utilitarianism wasn't cosmic or historical; it was about weights and measures. Jeremy Bentham—and, more recently, John Stuart Mill—had argued that people should make choices which maximize pleasure and avoid harm. It was a kind of bureaucratic ethics, concerned more with quantifying than understanding goodness. Carlyle likened its grinding out of pleasure to the workings of a *mill*—he liked puns—and said that it left no space for heroes or "strong men," those people who knew "what is doing" and actively pushed humanity forward. He compared utilitarianism's pencil-pushing with Muhammed's final judgment. At this point, Mill, who was in the audience, finally stood up and shouted "No!"[26]

Carlyle thought that men like Thomas Cromwell and Napoleon were "the modellers, patterns, and in a wide sense creators, of whatsoever the general mass of men contrived to do or to attain."[27] They didn't stoop to avoid harm, nor did they emerge from the general pattern. They wove the patterns others followed.

In *The Matrix Reloaded*, Neo flies off after a fight scene and a character called Link says, "He's doing his Superman thing." Like Carlyle's hero, he is consumed by a mission only he can fulfill. Everyone else is superfluous because his power comes from within, burning on the fuel of ego alone. What makes the strongman strong is his rejection of others. He *does*, while they watch.

I t's probably not surprising that, in valorizing the Self, Carlyle turned violently against the Other. In 1849, sixteen years after Britain abolished slavery, he wrote an *Occasional Discourse on the Negro Question.*

In it, Carlyle warned the world against the perils of abolition—this was fourteen years before Lincoln would sign the Emancipation Proclamation—describing black freedmen in Jamaica "with their beautiful muzzles up to their ears in pumpkins . . . while the sugar crops rot around them, uncut."[28] To his mind, these former slaves weren't at fault exactly. Like other beasts of burden, they inclined to torpor without the "beneficent whip."[29] So he directed most of his anger toward those Millian philanthropists and utilitarians who with "rosepink sentimentalism" and "all-bewildering jargon"[30]—words like *benevolence* and *fraternity*—had tried to persuade the public of a dangerous illusion: that pain might be abolished.

Since time immemorial, Carlyle wrote, the West Indies had "produced mere jungle, savagery, poison reptiles and swamp malaria," and they would have remained in that state without colonization. Of the native islanders, he went on to write, "till the white European first saw them, they were as if not yet created."[31]

The first settlers were heroes in the grand mold; they didn't just have a warrior's ability to subdue but could also create. With manful industry, they had tamed the "pestiferous jungle" and made it bear sweet sugar cane. In the face of such power, freedom and benevolence fell away.

eroes have been around since long before Western—let alone white—civilization. The earliest surviving epic poem, transcribed onto clay tablets over two thousand years before the birth of Christ, recounts the adventures of Gilgamesh and Enkidu, the strength of the latter "as mighty as a rock from the sky."[32]

For the Ancient Greeks, drawing on that much older tradition which merged the historical and supernatural, heroes were either gods themselves or, often, the mixed offspring of gods and mortals—demigods. Heracles and Achilles were demigods who drifted (sometimes uncomfortably) between worlds, performing feats that amazed humans and angered the heavens.

From the beginning of the *Iliad*, Achilles is vocal about his fate without being a slave to it. He remains in control, choosing the direction his life takes. Like him, Barack Obama is self-possessed and self-aware about his destiny. He has qualities of forbearance and force of will. His image is of a more conventionalized, mild-mannered Achilles.

Perhaps Keanu is a hero of a different, less obvious kind—

akin to sly, slippery Odysseus. A mortal king, Odysseus's super-power is described in the first line of Homer's epic poem: he is *polytropos*, a man of "many turns." Emily Wilson, the classics professor and recent translator of the *Odyssey*, argues that this word foregrounds the question of Odysseus's passivity. Is he "much turning" or "much turned"?[33] A trickster or himself easily tricked? Either way, his is a form of heroism that doesn't come from clubbing a hydra to death but from his extraordinary changeableness. In Wilson's translation, she calls him "compli-cated."[34]

"It's not my ambition to be an action hero," said Keanu in an interview with *The San Francisco Examiner* after the release of *Speed* in 1994. "To me it's an ensemble piece, not a hero piece. The protagonist isn't in the prow."[35]

More recently, in a conversation for *The Nerdist* podcast in 2017, Keanu talks about how he often plays "very reactive" characters.[36] Doesn't this show, says the interviewer, that they could be anyone, that anyone could become an *Übermensch* or superman? Keanu says "only through the struggle," which does sound quite Nietzschean. But what he's trying to emphasize, I think, is that most of his heroes, rather than being in control, are manically trying to keep up. They lack that sense of already-accomplished greatness you'd associate with a superman.

Keanu relates this to the character of John Wick, a contract killer who, in spite of his superheroic gift for kicking ass, is none-theless constantly getting his ass kicked. "John Wick keeps dig-ging a deeper hole for John," he says. "It's that conundrum of, yeah, I want my self-agency, but in order to achieve it I'm compromising any possibility of that actually ever happening."[37]

John would rather retire peacefully and brood on the memory of his late wife, but people keep trying to kill him. And every person he disposes of is replaced by two more, and then four more with bigger guns (it's like that fight scene in *The Matrix Reloaded* where Neo has to fend off endlessly replicating CGI copies of Agent Smith).

This feels true to the snakes-and-ladders logic of the *Odyssey* and *Gilgamesh*. Not long after Odysseus sets sail back from Troy, he can see his home, Ithaca, glinting on the horizon, only for his ship to be blown off course. It takes him another ten years to travel the six hundred miles or so back across the Aegean.

Obama is always deliberate, his speeches mapping out a clear "journey" or "quest," whereas Keanu's heroes give us the sense that, in spite of their strength and guile, they're at the whim of the gods.

realize that I've been conflating Keanu's characters with Keanu himself. Personally, I don't mind. I think a large part of his appeal derives from the possibility his characters *might* really be him. He's one of only a few actors instantly recognizable by their first name and the way they talk (down to the pronunciation of the word *dude*).

He'd never be able to subsume himself in a real-life personality like Julian Assange or John Paul Getty III. Or, I'm sure he could, but what would be the point? Those are roles for actors desperate to show off their acting. The pleasure in watching Keanu is seeing him being Keanu.

So maybe it's no coincidence that over the course of his career he's played eight characters named John and an alien called Klaatu (which sounds a lot like Keanu). Most of his characters have an almost interchangeable quality, both with each other and the actor who plays them.

There are also particular themes that bind his movies together. I like to keep track of the laced motifs of drowsiness and spiritual awakening: *My Own Private Idaho* starts with a close-up on the dictionary definition of "narcolepsy"; *Johnny Mnemonic*, set in the year 2021, begins with Keanu's character receiving a "wake-up call"; *Street Kings* begins with Keanu's alarm going off as he hides under the duvet; in *Little Buddha*, Siddhartha (played by Keanu) rides out of the palace on a white horse as a monk says, "his dream was ending and his long waking was begun"; and in *Point Break*, Keanu comes under the spell of a surfer called Bodhi, whose name in Sanskrit refers to the process of spiritual awakening.

Keanu's acting emphasizes sameness rather than difference, exploiting the blurred line between his on- and off-screen personas. And the evasiveness of his interviews—where he seems not to care especially whether people think he's like Ted from *Bill & Ted's Excellent Adventure*—adds to this blurred impression. As with Odysseus, he knows his control over himself is partial.

In this essay, I quote from interviews with Keanu, dialogue spoken by Keanu's characters, and speeches by Obama. Of course, I know that Obama is real in a way Keanu's characters aren't, but the Keanu-composite in my head—formed over years of watching and living with his characters—feels as real to me, to the extent that it would be strange to treat it as purely fictional. His dialogue could have been performed by other actors, but those characters wouldn't exist in the same way.

And perhaps that says something about how racialization works. The color of your skin and your personal attributes may be theoretically separate—as a writer, I can hide behind language, constructing a narrative that floats free of my identity—

but, in reality, they're inextricable. Wherever I go, I'm read as a person of color. And this experience ends up seeping back into my writing. I can't escape myself. So when I watch movies I can't help but mentally flip between actors and the characters they play, between real-life and made-up, because it's true of how I see the world.

After Donald Trump's election victory in 2016, the historian Perry Anderson wrote an essay in the *New Left Review* arguing for a certain continuity between Obama and Trump, in that, though only one of them courted it as an end in itself, both were celebrities. And in Anderson's terms, "celebrity is not leadership, and is not transferrable. The personality it projects allows no diffusion. Of its nature, it requires a certain isolation."[38]

The problem for Obama, by Anderson's account, was that his personality was so overwhelming. He was convinced of his fate, driven by a sense that this was his "defining moment."[39] And when he left office, it became clear that others thought so too; according to Gallup polling, he had the joint-fourth highest final approval ratings of any departing president. But the glow of his charisma no longer extended to the rest of the Democratic Party.

In December of 2009, the House of Representatives was made up of 257 Democrats and 178 Republicans (the largest majority since Jimmy Carter); by November 2016, the Republicans had 247 seats to the Democrats' 188. For Anderson, this was all too predictable. Obama had relished "his aura" and, rather than dilute it, "reserved the largesse showered on him by big money for further acclamation at the polls." As a result, his "celebrity dazzled, but didn't convert."[40] It clung to him like a shiny frock coat.

In defense of his record—and dazzled in turn—celebrities like Jay-Z said of Obama, "He's not a superhero." [41] The fact that his defense would even be couched in these terms shows the extent of Obama's problem. From the beginning, he seemed to know it. Eighteen days before the 2008 election, at a fundraising dinner in New York, he joked that "contrary to the rumors you have heard, I was not born in a manger. I was actually born on Krypton and sent here by my father, Jor-El, to save the planet Earth." [42]

In March 2011, this joke was taken at face value when Trump started calling on him to present his birth certificate to the American public and prove that he wasn't actually an alien. Those among the right-wing media who already hated Obama harped relentlessly on his identity, fixating on his "demonic" appearance and supposed links to the Black Panthers, as well as the authorship of his memoir, which some claimed was ghost-written by a white man.[43]

Any statement that tried to shift the debate back to policy was soon framed around him as a person, an isolated personality. To some, he was a superhero; to others, a villain. Perhaps he knew that, as a black man in America called Barack, the only way he could succeed was to recast himself in the glowing mold of the hero. And in making that choice, he must have known that he would be destined like all heroes—even Achilles, in the end—to fall short.

Living an ocean away, I felt complicit in this failure. Back then, I saw him as someone in whom one places faith rather than support. I couldn't see that, though his globe-spanning, mixed-race story was exceptional, he was still a politician: well-intentioned, but flawed and constrained.

Thinking I had found a hero, I experienced something new at Obama's success: *relief*, the sensation of a burden being lifted that I hadn't realized was there. I think this is one of the functions of superheroes. They come to represent—to manifest—what is by definition beyond our ability. They take away the weight of our own expectations.

arlyle said he found "a Portrait superior in real instruction to half-a-dozen written 'Biographies.'"[44] Portraits aren't beholden to sense in the way that words and syntax are; they can instruct before they're understood. Or perhaps, as Lao-Tzu puts it, the problem with words is that "nothing that can be said in words is worth saying."[45]

In researching this essay, I've scrolled through dozens of images of Keanu and Obama trying to work out what instruction their faces offer. What do their faces say about the kinds of hero they are?

Keanu's face hasn't changed much over the years. At the beginning of his career, he was floppy-haired and clean-shaven. Now he sports a neat beard and a middle parting. Slightly looser around the jowls and grizzlier, his glare is steely as ever, and his downturned mouth unsmiling though not unfriendly. That expression of faraway bafflement remains the same. As a hero, he seems to deflect the viewer's gaze outward and beyond.

Obama's hair has whitened over the last decade, and his eyes are baggier and darker-ridged—this last feature is most noticeable when he frowns. Looking at images of him, you notice how radically his face changes depending on his mood. He can guffaw and mimic, lark around and contort his upper body for emphasis, which gives those moments when he shrinks back into himself to address a serious issue—the laughter lines uncreasing and brows narrowing—an unadorned power. As a hero, he seems to draw the viewer's gaze more deeply inward.

In looking at the faces of others, I've also looked more at my own. As a child I enjoyed tracing the downward curves of my eyelids, the in-slope of my nose, but from my early teens onward I started to avoid mirrors. My hair grew longer and messier as a result. If I look at myself now—at the asymmetrical droop of my eyes, the puffiness of my cheeks—I find it hard to keep my own gaze.

What "real instruction" have I derived from my own face and those of others? Two kinds of faces exist: the first you're born with, whose history precedes you; and the second you grow into, marked by vanity and self-loathing, care and neglect.

Heroes have the second kind of face, able to make their own history. The rest of us—the majority—fail to escape the shadow of the first and so live between the two. We look in the mirror—awkwardly, critically—and recoil. It's easier to take up the faces of heroes which, outside of ourselves and perfect, we can wear like masks.

This feeling must have been behind Nietzsche's construction of his *Über* alter ego Zarathustra. In one of his saddest aphorisms, Nietzsche asks this lonely question: "Wanderer, who are you?" The wanderer-figure stands in for the author: placeless and unknown, desperate for something but unsure what. Offered refreshment, he rejects it and asks instead for "One more mask! A second mask!" The wanderer is beyond self-knowledge, or self-knowledge is beyond him. His only hope is a second mask.

For people of color, the body is inescapable, and pride in it never far from disgust. In the seventeenth and eighteenth centuries, the concept of separate, hierarchically ordered "races" had yet to be fully articulated. Adherence to the Bible meant that we must all, to some degree, be members of the same human family, however warped by foreign climes.[46]

In the mid-seventeenth century, François Bernier, traveler and physician, became one of the first to classify humans without reference to the children of Noah. After seeing Africans in Turkish and Arabian slave markets, he described them as having distinctively thick lips and oily skin. Chinese and Southeast Asians, by contrast, had "little pig eyes, long and deep-set."[47] Both were notable for their three or four tufts of beard.

This last detail might seem especially odd, but the Victorian naturalist Charles Hamilton Smith would later obsess over hair as a signifier of racial type, dividing humans into "Caucasian or Bearded," "Mongolians or Beardless," and "Wooly Haired or Tropical."[48] And soon a horde of ethnologists, biologists, and craniometrists would rush to find new ways of proving the superiority of the white European race, be it Caucasian, Aryan, or Nordic. Long before that point, though, it was taken for granted that to be white was the apex. In the words of Arthur de Gobineau, the white race "possessed the monopoly of beauty, intelligence and strength."[49]

When Carl Linnaeus, the famous Swedish lover of lists, wrote his *Systema Naturae* in 1735, splitting the natural world up into kingdoms, families, and orders, he defined *Simia* (monkeys) and *Bradypus* (sloths) by their physical characteristics (focusing on teeth especially), but chose not to define humans anatomically. Their most distinctive feature, he said—their "Providential gift"[50]—was reason, so next to HOMO he wrote simply *Nosce te ipsum*. Know yourself.

He did, however, list four "varieties" of human you could know yourself to be: European, American, Asian, and African. In 1758, he added more detail, claiming that Americans were red, bilious, and governed by "customs"; Europeans white, sanguine, and governed by "laws"; Asians basan (a yellowy, tanned sheepskin color), melancholic, and governed by "opinion"; while Africans were black, phlegmatic, and governed by "chance."[51]

Though this taxonomy was new, it drew on the ancient idea that the body was made up of a balance of substances called humors, which affected temperament and health. So if Asians were melancholic, that meant their dominant humor was black bile, secreted from the gallbladder.

In Linnaeus's time, "race" was seen more often in terms of families and horses rather than people. Even in the 1840s, Charles Dickens could still refer to the Chuzzlewit family as a "race."[52] This older definition of race saw it not as an immutable brand—able to identify you at first meeting—but a set of inherited characteristics, fluid and changeable over time. By the mid-nineteenth century, however, cracks were appearing in the unity of God's creation.

In *Coningsby*, a novel by future Prime Minister Benjamin Disraeli, a character called Sidonia is obsessed with the idea of a pure Caucasian race, "perceptible in its physical advantages, and in the vigour of its unsullied idiosyncrasy." By contrast, all "mixed races" seem destined to "wear away and disappear," lacking the requisite "vigour" to compete.[53] Sidonia is the exponent of a new way of looking at race. For him, race is not a set of traits passed down within a family and changeable over time, but a fixed sign, the marker of a person's strength, virility, and purity.

By this view, one race is capable of being definitively sullied by its contact with another. Gobineau's *Essay on the Inequality of the Human Races* would give this as the reason for the rise and fall of civilizations: union with other varieties created "hybrids," causing "a confusion which, like that of Babel, ends in utter impotence, and leads societies down to the abyss of nothingness."[54] In *Mein Kampf*, Hitler would make a similar argument—it's often suggested he read Gobineau—about cultural decline: "the Aryan neglected to maintain his own racial stock unmixed and therewith lost the right to live in the paradise which he himself had created."[55] The mixed-race person was, by definition, fallen.

n *Dreams from My Father*, Obama recalls coming across a magazine article as a small boy: a man with "heavy lips and a broad, fleshy nose" had paid for chemical treatment to lighten his skin—to pass—and now he looked ill, his face a "ghostly hue." Seeing it, Obama's face turned hot. "My stomach knotted," he writes, "the type began to blur on the page." It was like being in a nightmare, with "no voice for my newfound fear."[56] It wasn't just that a medical procedure had gone horribly wrong, but that he was being made aware—for the first time—of his own face as wrong. Why else would someone want to mutilate it with chemical cream?

I felt a similar knot in my stomach when I first read about Dr. John Langdon Down in Michael Banton's *Racial Theories*. Down was the superintendent at a mental hospital called the Royal Earlswood Asylum for Idiots in the mid-nineteenth century. In 1866, he wrote a paper arguing that disease in parents could result in degeneracy in their children. According to prevailing scientific wisdom, the last stage of fetal development involved working through the various human types—Malay,

Negro, American, Mongolian—until, in the words of evolutionary scientist Robert Chambers, attaining the "highest or Caucasian type." So a Caucasian would be complete at birth, and a Mongolian—someone with typically East Asian features—"an arrested infant newly-born."[57]

Drawing on Chambers's 1866 paper, Down concluded that "a very large number of congenital idiots are typical Mongols. So marked is this, that when placed side by side, it is difficult to believe that the specimens are not children of the same parents." For around one hundred years, what's now known as Down syndrome was referred to as Mongolism.

In my school playground, "mong" was a standard insult, and though not explicitly racialized—there weren't enough East Asian–looking kids to make that stick—it carried the taint of racial thinking. Everyone would have agreed that East Asians looked the same, had less intelligent features, and aspired to a "Caucasian" ideal they could never achieve. One time, a kid from the year above pushed past me on the stairs grunting *mong*; another time, a kid in the year above stuck his tongue beneath his lower lip so that it bulged out and then pulled his eyes half-shut to grimace at me. I looked beyond him and walked on.

In 1924, the year before Hitler published the first volume of *Mein Kampf*, a Harvard-educated journalist and member of the Ku Klux Klan, Lothrop Stoddard, wrote a book called *Racial Realities in Europe*. In it, Stoddard declared that the melting-pot experiment was over. The United States had proven once and for all that racial heredity was what determines character. Just look at the accomplishments of people of "Nordic stock": they'd drawn up the Constitution, won the West, and made America into the world's most powerful nation. Liberals insisting on the country's "hybrid" character were deluded. To make America great again, the best thing the country could do was to stop trying to "absorb these refractory aliens."[58]

Stoddard thought there was friend and foe, Self and Other; there were sanguine, law-abiding whites and—to use Linnaeus's terminology—basan or phlegmatic savages. He closed his book with an exhortation: "Know thyself!"[59]

Looking for a picture of Stoddard online—side-slicked black hair and waxed moustache—I found a meme posted on the Neo-Nazi website Stormfront less than three months before

Trump's election victory. It showed Stoddard's face with the caption: "The September 11th attack would not have surprised this fellow."

Comments below described him as a "scientist and idealist." One commenter, "ForeverWhiteMan," wrote, "He seems to have been very accurate." Beneath ForeverWhiteMan's post, his signature included a toll-free number to report "mexican [*sic*] illegals."[60]

I knew, of course, that this was only one drop in an angry, paranoid ocean. And maybe it was just a coincidence that the first person to post the Stoddard meme had joined Stormfront in December 2015, six months after Trump announced his candidacy. But seeing the dates—looking at that low-res image of Stoddard's waxed moustache—I felt a familiar knot in my stomach.

n *47 Ronin*, Keanu plays a skilled swordsman consigned to the fringes of society, accused of being a demon and referred to constantly as "Half Breed." This role is unusual in a career during which he's scarcely played straightforwardly "ethnic" or racialized characters. At the same time, he's rarely been cast in the mold of a white, all-American hero. In *The Matrix* and *John Wick*, his characters seem to spring forth fully formed, unmoored from any family, at a remove from normal society.

And Keanu has often been racialized in subtle ways, described in interviews as "taciturn," "laconic," and "mysterious,"[61] or, as another character describes him in *Point Break*, "young, dumb, and full of cum." Less subtly, at the outset of his career in 1988, a *Los Angeles Times* article quoted the screenwriter and director Ron Nyswaner as saying of him: "He's like a Chinese menu."[62] This epithet and those others don't *necessarily* suggest racialization—Nyswaner would probably say he was unaware of Keanu's Hawaiian-Chinese heritage—but they do fit a pattern.

In David Remnick's biography of Obama, he writes about the tendency among scholars to treat Hawaii as "a kind of racial

Eden." He quotes from Romanzo Adams's *The Peoples of Hawaii*, which claimed there was "abundant evidence that the peoples of Hawaii are in a process of becoming one people."[63] The film professor R. L. Rutsky, in his essay "Being Keanu," has critiqued the long history of "Western portrayals of Hawaiian and Pacific Island cultures as Edenic paradises filled with beautiful, sensual natives, untroubled by depth or thought."[64]

This casts a specific light on comments like those of director Bernardo Bertolucci who once said, ruminating on Keanu's qualities: "There's this fantastic line about Henry James—I think it was T. S. Eliot who said it: 'His sublime mind was never violated by an idea,' meaning that James was beyond ideas."[65] But where Eliot was discussing James's fiction, Bertolucci is describing how he sees Keanu himself—his appearance, his speech, his acting. He is the sensual native, his mind unviolated by ideas—too in touch with the "sublime" (a word not used by Eliot) to express rational thought. Despite never having lived in Hawaii, Keanu struggles to escape its sensuous shadow.

E ven if you pass as white in most ways, or have a particularly complex heritage, stereotypes have a habit of catching up with you. In my own past, people have suggested that—in the vein of Ming the Merciless—I'm "impassive" or "cool", and they've extended those traits to my writing, describing it as unemotional and delicate as a fine silk print. When they do, it feels like a shadow has fallen across me. Or, worse, that the shadow was always there. I'd just been ignoring it.

In a 1991 interview, Keanu said of himself: "I'm a meathead. I can't help it, man. You've got smart people and you've got dumb people. You just happen to be spending some time with a dumb person."[66]

Has Keanu internalized racial thinking here, playing the part of the stereotypical Pacific Islander? Or would he simply prefer not to answer the interviewer's questions?

In 1995, rumors spread that Keanu had married the record executive David Geffen in a secret ceremony in Paris or on a beach in Mexico. "If sexual ambiguity was as easy to grow as tomatoes, he would be the biggest gardener in Hollywood!"[67] declared the French magazine *Voici*. In *Vanity Fair*, Michael Shnayerson suggested that it would be "useful to shoot the rumors down cold," asking directly whether or not Keanu was gay. "To deny it is to make a judgment," he replied, at which point Shnayerson changed the topic.[68]

The feminist is someone who "stops the smooth flow of communication,"[69] writes Sara Ahmed in *Living a Feminist Life*. In refusing to play by the rules of what Adrienne Rich called the "bias of compulsory heterosexuality,"[70] Keanu's evasions—intentionally or not—show how it might be possible to resist the fixed boundaries of masculine and racial identities.

In another interview—this time with *Premiere* magazine in 1994—Keanu was asked whether he had "consciously" tried to set himself apart from other male actors of his generation. "I mean, I've always played the kind of male equivalent of the female ingénue,"[71] he said.

Back at school, I saw Keanu as having the better, more acceptable version of my face—neither pig-eyed nor mongoloid—but maybe I was drawn to another of his qualities: his ability to slip *all* boundaries. In pitching himself as a "female ingénue"—refusing to comply with the rules of heteromasculinity—he reclaimed the space that racialization takes away. Calling yourself a "female ingénue," after all, belies ingenuousness; it suggests a kind of aesthetic self-consciousness. It also makes me think—which is another quality Keanu has cultivated—of the *inconnu*: the figure of someone unknown to others and so free to define themselves.

n a phenomenon that began under Obama's presidency, *The Matrix* has featured increasingly in Neo-Nazi and alt-right discourse. A popular subreddit, TheRedPill, run by an anonymous user calling themselves Morpheus Manfred, boasts almost 240,000 "unplugged" subscribers, providing a forum where men—and only men—can express themselves free from censure, to complain about uppity women and rail against a "feminized" culture that's swallowed the blue pill of political correctness.

In alt-right jargon, to "redpill" someone is to unplug them from the (Feminist? Islamist? Neo-Marxist?) Matrix, to wake them up to a reality that's white, male, and proud. If he were around today, Lothrop Stoddard would no doubt be another Morpheus Manfred, probably banned from Twitter but with a YouTube channel or an angry blog, spending his free time with other Proud Boys (an organization described on their website as being for "Western Chauvinists who refuse to apologize for creating the modern world"[72]). Whatever the case, Stoddard would be doing his best to redpill someone.

The alt-right vision is defined by its simplicity, its belief in its own correctness. In the world of *The Matrix*, there's a character called the Oracle. You might expect her to be similarly confident and self-assured in her judgments, maybe occupying a position of obvious power or influence. Instead, she's an elderly black woman living in a small apartment in a rough-looking neighborhood.

At a crucial moment in the first *Matrix* film, Neo goes to see her. He wants to find out if he's the One, the savior-like figure whose coming has been foretold. The Oracle is sitting in her kitchen smoking. She responds by pointing toward a wooden sign above her doorway, on which are printed the words *Temet Nosce*.

"You know what that means?" she asks. "It's Latin. Means, 'Know Thyself.' I'm gonna let you in on a little secret. Being the One is just like being in love. Nobody can tell you you're in love."

I was always puzzled by that "little secret." What does she mean? Is Neo meant to know instinctively that he's the One in the same way you know you're in love? But being in love is pretty much the most uncertain, tangled sort of knowledge there is. You can't know it in the way you can know if it's raining outside or if you have food on your face. It's too fitful, too complicated. If knowledge excludes room for doubt, maybe love can't be "known" at all.

Convinced of their ability to see through the delusions of others, the alt-right believe themselves uniquely in possession of self-knowledge. But as Nietzsche wrote, the self is "something that shall be overcome."[73]

At this stage in the journey, Neo is still too occupied with trying to work out who he is. The Oracle wants him to see that any certainty he's looking for—or thinks he wants—is not just impossible but a *bad idea.* Speaking from the perspective of what Audre Lorde calls the "dehumanized inferior,"[74] the Oracle knows how often the power of an assured self rests on the oppression of others. One person's certainty comes at the expense of another's freedom. But the self is something open and unknowable. Like love, identity should be founded on doubt.

To make her point, she pretends to be an orthodontist, examining the inside of Neo's mouth to check for signs of his Oneness. This is what he wants, right? Empirical certainty. As if teeth and gums might reveal his destiny, as if it were possible to discover your identity in the same way you might find out that you have gingivitis.

When we first meet Neo in *The Matrix* he's asleep at his desk—a recurring image in Keanu's movies—bathed in the light of his computer screen. A message bleeps. "What? What the hell?" he splutters. There's a knock at the door: "Something wrong, man? You look a little whiter than usual." In the original script, this character is called Choi ("a young Chinese man") but in the actual film Choi is played by a white guy.

It's not clear why Neo is so confused, but for most of the film he has a similar look on his face—the look of someone who hasn't quite woken up. On meeting him, Morpheus phrases it differently. He recognizes in Neo "the look of a man who accepts what he sees because he is expecting to wake up."

This look suggests that Neo knows the world around him isn't quite right but accepts its glitches nevertheless. Maybe he thinks they can't continue forever. However bad the dream, it has to end. This would be typical for a Keanu hero: not in the prow; strong yet passive; aware of things being wrong but not actively looking to set them right, or waiting for the right moment to present itself. Led rather than leading, he works by intuition, not force.

Morpheus, named after the god of sleep, has come to tell him that now is the time to wake up and act. In the Wachowskis' script, Morpheus is described as having "the unadulterated confidence of a zealot." Rather than staying to defend his homeland, he has ventured in search of the One. Thinking he's found him in Neo, he becomes his guide and mentor. Most of the film follows Morpheus's attempts to teach Neo how to overcome the Matrix, as when, in kung fu films, the master takes on a raw apprentice. Here, since the kung fu can be downloaded straight into Neo's brain, the purpose of his training isn't so much to teach him how to fight as to get him to see the world differently.

But Neo has spent his whole life in the Matrix, a system of control so all-consuming as to have structured every aspect of his experience. To reprogram him, Morpheus has to start at the very beginning. Neo must unlearn his most basic impulses before he can reach the point of jumping from a tall building—a part of his training—without any fear of falling, without even *expecting* to fall. He needs to become a different person: a more fluid, mixed version of himself.

first watched *The Matrix* on VHS in 2000. My dad had just bought a PC made by a short-lived computer manufacturer called Tiny which loomed over one half of our living room. While I sat on the other side of the room, in front of the TV watching *The Matrix*'s opening sequence—a loud gunfight and chase scene—I had to listen over the sound of computer cooling fans whirring menacingly in the background.

The disparity between the machines depicted in the film—capable of battery-farming the whole human species—and our own, barely capable of spider solitaire, should have been glaring. But in the light of *The Matrix*, our massive Tiny seemed to radiate a sense of possibility.

Keanu, too, radiated possibility. More than one and less than two, as Donna Haraway had it; or, as his friend Tirzah said, he was the kind of hero who could be "anything you wanted him to be." When I went on our PC for the first time, basking in the white light of its screen, I had that same feeling as I did watching *The Matrix*, imagining myself as Neo. It was like entering a new, borderless world.

One of the few surviving fragments of the pre-Socratic philosopher Heraclitus says: "the one is made up of all things, and all things issue from the one."[75] A version of this sentiment appears on U.S. coins in Latin—*e pluribus unum*—and was the United States' unofficial motto for years, summing up the shared hopes of a single nation patched together from numerous states. This ideal is also inscribed into the meaning of the word *individual*, which originally referred to the Trinity: the three divine persons that make up the indivisible One.

Though Keanu is perfect as Neo, there's something ironic about him being the "One." He's complicated, a man of many turns; his kind of celebrity is characterized by its diffuseness. Instantly recognizable—he can't eat a sandwich in public without becoming a meme—and yet somehow inscrutable. Maybe it makes more sense to see him as the point at which the One and the Many (or Self and Other) meet. His aim, as he said in an interview with *Detour Magazine* in 1993, is "to fall into all categories—and no categories!"[76]

A gent Smith is Neo's mirror image. Where Neo is an anomaly, uncertain and rebellious, Smith is power in all its vestiges— white, male, state-sanctioned. More than that, he's filled with a visceral disgust for humans. So while the other agents are anonymous men in suits, trained to fight the resistance with the bland efficiency of anti-virus software, he takes it personally.

Toward the end of the first film, when Morpheus is being tortured, Smith leans in close. It looks like he's about to lick the sweat from off his forehead. "This zoo," says Smith. "This prison. This reality, whatever you want to call it, I can't stand it any longer . . . It's the smell, if there is such a thing. I feel saturated by it. I can taste your stink and every time I do, I fear that I've somehow been infected by it."

On the tip of his tongue is the kind of racial slur that would place this scene in the prison cell of any number of anti-colonial fighters, civil rights activists, or Free South Africa protesters from throughout the twentieth century, or further back. In 1652, when Europeans first settled on the Cape of Good Hope, a white settler recorded his first impressions of the Khoikhoi people: "The local natives have everything in common with the dumb cattle, barring their human nature . . . They all smell fiercely."[77]

Perhaps the Wachowskis were making a point in their casting. Neo is open and unreadable, able to pass in a way that Morpheus, who is black, cannot. In spite of this—and the many styles of kung fu he masters—he can't win by the rules. Agent Smith is not killable. As soon he dies, he reappears in the place of someone else plugged into the Matrix. Every onlooker is a potential informant, a body into which he can switch.

Morpheus's task is to make Neo aware of the Matrix, to convince him that what might appear absolute and infallible is nothing of the sort. "You have to let it all go, Neo. Fear, doubt and disbelief." But you can't just be told this kind of thing.

The lesson Neo finally learns is to stop trying. Instead of trying to be stronger and faster than Smith, he simply leaps headfirst into his chest—a move that recalls his earlier practice at jumping off buildings. As Smith's body shatters from within into a hundred tiny pieces of badly rendered CGI—apparently rewriting his code—the symbolism is clear: Neo is penetrating him. Smith's face contorts with horror, or with the complex self-disgust of the white Southerner who, having ranted about the dangers of race pollution, finds himself in bed with a Chinaman.

This is mixedness as an explosive force, a special power: the Mixed-Race Superman become a strong wind bursting open the angry, controlling certainties of white manhood.

Even though *The Matrix* was released in 1999, part of its enduring appeal is that it feels like a post-9/11 film—a film for now. It responds to the lurking chaos, the grotesque inequality, beneath the flat surface of Western society. David Cronenberg's *eXistenZ*, also released in 1999, channels a similar fear, depicting a world in which participants can play out their darkest fantasies in immersive video games. In both movies, order is constructed; the threat of rupture looms. Power can only stay hidden for so long.

was born in 1989, the year that Obama started at Harvard Law School and Keanu starred in *Bill & Ted's Excellent Adventure.*

Elsewhere, the Berlin Wall was reduced to rubble and Nicolae Ceaușescu executed as protests flared in Tiananmen Square and Czechoslovakia. The Soviet Union, holding its first elections since 1917, was edging toward collapse. But while the established order trembled, power in the United States was being passed smoothly from one Republican president to another. Chaos abroad only served to confirm U.S. hegemony. And for the next twelve years at least, the West would pretend that no other future had been possible and nothing uncertain. History was dead. In its wake—laughing into the sunset—was white, liberal democracy.

Looking back, the United States' swaggering '90s pose can be seen—or pre-empted—in the previous decade's movies. 1989 was an especially blockbuster year. Movies like *Indiana Jones and the Last Crusade, Batman, Ghostbusters II,* and *Lethal Weapon 2* contributed to box-office takings of over $1 billion in the US alone. American superhero-strongmen were everywhere, lassoing and shooting their way across the screen. Reckless or roguish, each controlled their fate. In *Dead Poets Society*, another movie from 1989, Robin Williams's character John Keating sums up the mood: "Hear it? Carpe. Carpe diem. Seize the day, boys. Make your lives extraordinary."

On their excellent adventure, Bill and Ted have two mottos that echoed through my childhood: "be excellent to each other" and "party on." In the '90s, it felt like everyone in the West had agreed on their final, mutual excellence and now just wanted to party on. In keeping with this, the house I grew up in was washed of any reminders of my Indonesianness, my otherness. It was easier for my mum to forget, and hope I would too. Difference, if I noticed it or if it appeared, took the attractive form of those mixed-race couples on billboards for United Colors of Benetton. Or it was the cute interracial kids hugging at the end of the music video for Michael Jackson's "Heal the World." It was never hard or hateful or ugly.

Which must be why when, in 1999, the Macpherson Report—commissioned by New Labour to assess the shortcomings of the Stephen Lawrence investigation—was finally published, though there were the usual blandishments (Tony Blair said it would lead to a "fundamental shift in the way British society deals with racism"[78]), it was mostly ignored or criticized.

Michael Gove, later to hold a variety of senior public posts—including Secretary of State for Education, Justice, and the Environment—was a journalist then, and used his column in *The Times* to rage against "race radicals" and what he called "a new McCarthyism."[79] A few weeks after Stephen's death, in

March 1993, the *Daily Mail* had covered a march demanding justice for Stephen, which they described as "unrest . . . fomented for political motives." The protesters were nothing more than "race militants."[80]

Just as the *Daily Mail* criticized anti-racist groups for turning "the brutal killing of a schoolboy into a political cause,"[81] so Gove claimed the Macpherson Report was fundamentally "illiberal." The proper way to support minority communities, he wrote, was through the invisible hand of economic opportunity and personal freedom. He subscribed to a neoliberal creed that worshipped personal choice and the free market above all else. It meant that the death of an individual, however outrageous the systemic failures that led to it and prevented justice from being served, could only be seen in terms of bad individual choices.

Gove also expressed concern at the recommendations put forward by the Commission on the Future of Multi-Ethnic Britain, launched by Lord Parekh and the Runnymede Trust in 1997 (which published its recommendations in 2000). The Commission proposed diversity quotas for public appointments, tactics to reduce discrimination in schools, and ethnic minority recruitment targets for private franchises. "They are orders for a forced march down one path," wrote Gove, "paved with good intentions, towards a massive and illiberal extension of state power."[82]

In *The Times*, Gove laid out his dream for Martin Luther King's "colour-blind society"—before suggesting that those who supported the report of Lord Parekh's Commision were comparable to "apartheid's apologists."[83] It was this same overwhelming confidence—in the free market, in liberal democracy—that had propelled Tony Blair to power. Hope was closing your eyes to color. And history, if you didn't look behind or beneath you, could be seen anew, unmarred by the wreckage of discrimination. It was a path down which, in spite of occasional diversions, we all marched hand-in-hand toward a better, more excellent future.

When he ran for office, many held Barack Obama up as evidence of how far society had come, of a new "colorblind" or "post-racial" politics.[84] In hindsight, he seems to hark back to the world as described by Carlyle in his lectures on heroism, with the Great Man a fixed point, a "living rock amid all rushings-down."[85] Without heroes, the world was "bottomless and shoreless." Great Men gave purpose to history, laying down markers through their great acts that others could follow.

As the confidence of the '90s gave way to the uncertainty of the '00s, trailing the wreckage of terror attacks and foreign wars and economic crashes, it was easy to feel adrift. Where was the living rock amid the flux?

In 2008, new age-guru Deepak Chopra said that "the X factor which sets Barack Obama aside as a unique candidate is his hard-won self-awareness."[86] In knowing himself, decreed Chopra, Obama could set the United States on "the journey back to self-awareness as a people." As much a spiritual as a political leader, Obama raised the possibility of "a quantum leap in American consciousness."[87] For Chopra, Obama was that self-knowing man, modeler and pattern to others, the rock on whom so many hopes rested.

A number of journalists and commentators sought to place Obama historically, crediting him with a special ability—like Lincoln or Roosevelt—to understand his political moment, but perhaps his real skill was this more mystical ability to project self-knowledge.

In *The Seven Spiritual Laws of Superheroes*, Chopra goes into more detail about the ways in which heroes can change the world, one of them being to master "creativity." He uses the analogy of the "imaginal cells" in a caterpillar which, at a certain point, begin to rebel against the insect's normal cells, "replicating and spreading." This violent back-and-forth—or dialectical movement, though Chopra doesn't quote Hegel or Marx—is what gives way to a new synthesis, all of the clustered cells working together as "the actual transformation takes place—a caterpillar takes the quantum leap and becomes something entirely new and innovative, a beautiful butterfly."[88]

New Labour claiming that society had "changed fundamentally" only conveyed a sense of urgent vagueness, whereas when Obama spoke about his own mixed story he embodied change in himself, butterfly-like. His certain and self-knowing masculinity was the evidence of change's possibility.

Obama launched his first campaign for president the year I started university, in 2007. At the time, I remember reading Coleridge's description of the imagination as the "infinite I AM."[89] Half-understanding what he meant, I thought it sounded like a new age mantra, a command to place your private experience in a cosmic perspective. Or, more blasphemously, to re-make the universe in your own image, stamping your identity ("I AM I AM") on every rock, tree, and puddle.

But watching Obama on the campaign trail, Coleridge's words made an abrupt sense. Obama knew himself, and when he spoke, the "imaginal" and "normal" cells of politics, previously disordered, rearranged themselves around him. For a moment, I could see the world—for all its flagrant chaos and violence—through his awed experience of it, personal and infinite.

In *Dreams from My Father*, there is a recurring pattern whereby Obama's growing sense of conviction is sharpened in opposition to the confusions and self-delusions of others, and the book's two main encounters with other mixed-race people fit squarely within this narrative.

The first encounter happens in 1979. In his freshman year at Occidental College, Obama meets a green-eyed, mixed-race student named Joyce and suggests they go to a Black Students' Association meeting together. She's affronted. "I'm not black," she says. "I'm *multiracial*." She has an Italian father and a mother who's part African, French, and Native American. "Why should I have to choose between them?" she asks.

Obama is affronted in turn—angry, even—but then he reflects on the similarities between Joyce's response and his own earlier, more immature attitude.

Unlike her, he stopped advertising his mother's race when he was around twelve, suspecting that, whether or not it was conscious, the reason he was telling white people was to ingratiate himself with them. He mentions the split-second adjustments of strangers, searching his eyes for evidence of a divided soul, for "the ghostly image of the tragic mulatto trapped between two worlds."

Going against the grain of people's assumptions, highlighting a proximity to whiteness when you don't pass as white, generates a special sort of anxiety. In my experience, the response to hearing about my mixed heritage—besides surprise, usually muted—is often tinged with pleasure. You go from being purely other to only partly so. Which is why it can be discomforting to say that my dad grew up in Devon. To emphasize that part of myself feels like erasing the other. I feel too few and too many.

No one should have to choose between their parents or the different parts of their heritage, but what I think Obama's college friend Joyce reacts to—what upsets her so much—is that the choice has already been made for her. However many times she says *multiracial* or *mixed race*, she can't choose how to be seen.

So when Obama identifies her as black, expecting the same acknowledgment in return, she balks at it because it reminds her of how little choice she's ever had. No longer Emerson's dreamed-of "transparent eyeball,"[90] unseen and observing, she becomes a body. A body that feels unreal to her. Alien.

The second encounter takes place in 1988. A 27-year-old Obama has flown to Nairobi to meet his Kenyan family. By coincidence, his half-brother Mark—studying physics at Stanford—is also visiting. They decide to go to an Indian restaurant and during the meal Obama asks him how he feels about Kenya.

"I don't feel much of an attachment. Just another poor African country," says Mark.

"I should have stopped then," Obama writes in his memoir, "but something—the certainty in this brother's voice, maybe, or our rough resemblance, like looking into a foggy mirror—made me want to push harder."

He asks his brother if he ever feels like he's "losing something," but Mark is smart. He can see where this is going: "You think I'm somehow cut off from my roots, that sort of thing."

They've had the same experience of an absent father, but where it makes Obama "mad" it only leaves Mark "numb."

Mark defends his numbness. Beethoven's symphonies and Shakespeare's sonnets still move him. "Who's to tell me what I should and shouldn't care about?"

For Mark, like Joyce, having a mixed identity means not being told what he should like, being able to choose. "Understand, I'm not ashamed of being half Kenyan. I just don't ask myself a lot of questions about what it all means. About who I *really* am."

Obama sees his brother hesitate for a moment, "like a rock climber losing his footing," before he recovers and asks the waiter for the bill. "What's certain," says Mark, "is that I don't need the stress."

Mark has closed off a part of his experience, turning away from his father's heritage. Looking at him is not just like looking in a foggy mirror—his way of thinking is itself foggy. Obama, though, sees him with the same ruthless clarity he would apply to making his own identity, as just another confused brother in denial about his past.

I n 1917, J. A. Rogers, a mixed-race Jamaican writer living in Harlem, published an unusual novella called *From Superman to Man.*[91]

Set on a train hurtling west from the snowy fields of Iowa to sun-kissed California, it recounts a four-day conversation between a black railway porter named Dixon and an unnamed racist state senator. Angry at having been drawn into argument—at having his prejudices challenged—the senator rants about cannibalism, slavery, and Shakespeare. Dixon listens patiently, responding at length with a host of quotations furnished from scientific journals, anthropology, and literature.

Dixon is exceptional: he speaks French and Spanish, has studied at Yale, fought in the war, and believes, with a passion that exceeds the senator's racism, in the "universality of human nature."

As the landscape thaws so does the senator, and by the time they reach California he has undergone a Scrooge-like epiphany. Not only does he reject his former views but vows to end the "great wrong" of racism.

"I never did realize until now," the senator says, "the great injustice that is being done to certain American citizens, and also the vast amount of ignorance that we, Caucasians, have to combat in our own people." He asks Dixon to come to Hollywood so that together they can make motion pictures popularizing a better understanding of race, and the two men shake hands "cordially."

This volte-face is ridiculous, but then so is Dixon—a fantastically superior being, purpose-built for the task of deconstructing racism.

From Superman to Man's title can be read in two ways: as tracking the senator's change of heart—his initial picture of the Nordic superman stripped of its superiority—or as suggesting that the book itself is addressed from a superman to a man, which is how it reads.

But why should the person of color have to be so wise and reasonable, so superhuman? I don't feel empowered by Dixon and I'm not convinced that, in his words, "the full light of justice will yet dawn." Mired in fantasy, justice seems further away than ever. Reading Rogers's narrative, I think of times I've had to listen quietly while being patronized or talked down to—"So you're cashing in on your roots?" "Isn't 'cultural appropriation' a fad?"—aware that if I argue back it will only extend the torture. I'm angry on Dixon's behalf, and I'm angry *at* him.

In 1905, the Irish playwright George Bernard Shaw's *Man and Superman* was performed in London and New York. In one version of Rogers's book he calls Shaw the truth-disseminating "salt of the intellectual world."[92] Both Shaw and Rogers shared an unwavering faith in progress and the supermen—powered by intellect and will, not race—who would lead it.

Shaw was a Fabian socialist, set on exposing the oppression of marriage and the hypocrisy of the ruling classes. Unlike Rogers, though, he wasn't enamored of democracy. He couldn't trust that knowing the "way to better things" was enough; it took a special individual charged with "Life Force" to reject what was wrongly deemed dutiful and just. His version of Nietzsche's *Übermensch* was fearless, leonine, and naysaying.

Hovering behind Shaw's hero-worship is the specter of eugenics, or as the hero of his play Jack Tanner calls it, "intelligently controlled, conscious fertility."[93] If you put your faith in the radical intervention of the individual, then what more radical intervention is there than manipulating the gene pool? If you believe that history is shaped by individuals, why not try to breed one from the strongest and most powerful stock?

As Rogers was writing his own intellectual emancipation, the kind of individual greatness he believed in was being used to argue in favor of breeding out impure stocks of "Africans" and "Mongols," and the cult of the Nordic superman was taking hold in Europe and America. Dixon is nevertheless unshaken in his belief that the right argument might show this all to be a terrible mistake, a small digression in the course of our journey toward mutual understanding. For all that his conviction is beautiful and worthy of admiration, he is full of the tragic naiveté which precedes a fall.

The story goes that after a day of studying, Barack Senior had gone to join his wife's father and some of his friends at a bar in Honolulu when a white man came up to the bartender and said—loud enough that everyone could hear—"I shouldn't have to drink good liquor next to a nigger."[94]

The room fell silent. Rather than getting angry, Barack walked over to the man and started to explain, slowly and evenly, the concept of universal rights. The man at the bar soon felt bad—so bad, in fact, that not only did he apologize but he gave Barack a hundred dollars on the spot, which paid for drinks and pupus all night and for the rest of his month's rent.

Obama says he didn't believe this story until, years later, he got a phone call from a man who said he'd studied with his father in Hawaii and he told him the same anecdote. In his voice, says Obama, "I heard the same note that I'd heard from Gramps so many years before, that exact note of disbelief—and hope."[95]

Hope runs counter to belief, or in spite of it. Though it's been raining for hours, I hope the sun will come out. Some part of me hopes to endure beyond the death of my body. Here, as religious faith would once have done, the system of rights provides the framework for conversion. The magic of universal rights—"the foundation of freedom, justice and peace in the world,"[96] as the United Nations puts it—imbues Barack Senior with a semi-religious fervor. He, in turn, embodies those rights, filling them with purpose. The spirit of fraternity, which would otherwise seem abstract and ghostly, is transformed into flesh and blood.

Or, only momentarily. Obama is full of awe retelling this story, but it makes me think of Dixon, of all the energy put into arguing back which, though it may not take its toll in the present, surely will in the future.

In 1964, after graduating from Harvard, Barack Senior returned to Kenya and got a high-ranking job at the Ministry of Economic Planning and Development. By 1967, though, two American friends came to visit his comfortable government-owned cottage and, according to Remnick's biography, found him chain-smoking and drinking quadruple shots of Vat 69 or Johnnie Walker. They thought Barack's decline was "at least partly related to the disappointed belief that the best would rise to the top."[97] Kenyan independence in 1963 had promised a new start: representative democracy; strong national industries; trade unions. But by the late '60s the Kenya African National Union was drifting toward one-party rule, with cronyism and corruption on the rise. Barack, sidelined because of his outspokenness, was crushed.

Or, less charitably perhaps, he had spent his life up until then succeeding—whether academically, or at what Obama called "womanizing"[98]—and, in post-colonial Kenya, he came up against forces he could neither master nor submit himself to. So he went out drinking and ranted against the government, ensuring his failure. In 1982, he had just been at an old colonial bar in Nairobi when he crashed into a gum tree and died. "I want to do things to the best of my ability," he had said. "Even when death comes, I want to die thoroughly."[99] He believed that reason might conquer history, that intellect and eloquence could overcome ignorance. But once the smoke cleared, what remained?

"There is a phrase in Indonesian, *diam dalam seribu bahasa*," Obama's half-sister Maya tells David Remnick, "that means 'to be silent in a thousand languages.' It's a very fitting phrase for this country."[100]

In 1967, when Obama was six years old, his mother Ann took him to Jakarta to live with her second husband, Lolo, who worked as an army geologist surveying roads and tunnels, and later as a liaison with the government for Union Oil. In Hawaii, Lolo had been fun and talkative, but in Indonesia he became withdrawn and started drinking more.

There were hints that Lolo had either seen things or somehow been involved in the events of 1965. That year, a military coup led by General Suharto—backed by the CIA—had toppled the country's president and founding father Sukarno. Shifting blame onto the Indonesian Communist Party, Suharto incited a countrywide purge of the Left, and over the next year there were violent reprisals in towns and villages across the country, spilling into full-blown slaughter when the Chinese community were singled out. This was partly because of their loose association with Communist China and partly because they were a minority who had always been held in suspicion. The Chinese, resident—and persecuted—in Indonesia since the sixteenth century, were killed in the hundreds of thousands.

Remnick, in his account, says that not long after arriving in Jakarta Ann came across a field of unmarked graves and asked Lolo about it. He was unresponsive. In Obama's memoir, he describes how Lolo had started to rebuff Ann when she asked what was wrong with him: "It was as if he had come to mistrust words somehow. Words, and the sentiments words carried."[101]

Obama's way of putting this reminds me of my mum's family, of the thousandfold silence surrounding what happened in the mid-sixties. My grandma was living on the east coast of Sumatra then. Her husband was arrested; friends disappeared. It was a long time ago, she used to say. After my grandad was released from prison he took the family to Jakarta, leaving Sumatra for the relative anonymity of the capital. My grandma lived there until her death, many years after him. When asked, she would say that she was never scared. It was hard to get more out of her than that.

Talking about Lolo, Obama fixates on "power" and how "words" might be used to conquer it. Barack Senior, the father he never knew, thought he could stand up to power. Like Dixon, his education and natural eloquence—his way with words—enabled him to humiliate those who would have power over him. Lolo was different. Lacking that same verbal fluency and mistrusting words anyhow, he crumpled at the first sign of pressure.

Without the power to talk, Lolo fell silent. Later, Obama

would conclude that this silence—the incapacity to describe what he'd seen—was what made him powerless.

I don't know if Lolo deserves pity—whether he was defeated by his circumstances or brought defeat upon himself—but I resent, on his behalf, the injunction to be superhuman. Stories like that of Barack Senior may be inspiring but speaking out doesn't necessarily confer power on the speaker. And not everyone *can* speak out. For my grandma, as for thousands of others living in Indonesia in the '60s, silence was a matter of survival. A response to extreme danger, requiring courage and work, it wasn't just a form of self-preservation but a means of protecting others.

"Language cannot do everything," writes Adrienne Rich in her poem "Cartographies of Silence," "chalk it on the walls where the dead poets / lie in their mausoleums."[102]

In March 2008, when Obama and Hillary Clinton were still fighting over the Democratic nomination, a number of incendiary recordings were leaked to the press. In them, Obama's old pastor from Chicago, the Reverend Jeremiah Wright—the man who had performed Barack and Michelle's marriage ceremony—was critical of US foreign policy and the legacy of white supremacy, calling the United States a racist country and shouting: "God damn America!"[103]

It was as if someone had suddenly unmuted the TV. Hysteria ensued. Clinton remarked that Wright "would not have been my pastor"[104] (which was hardly surprising). She asked Obama if by attending Trinity Church he had endorsed Wright's views? Behind all the "rosepink sentimentalism"—to use Carlyle's phrase—of Hope and Change, what did he really think? The pressure built on Obama to justify himself, to do what he had not done and talk explicitly about race.

The speech he gave was called "A More Perfect Union." Standing in front of a shimmering blue velvet curtain interspersed with the Stars and Stripes, he drew again on his mixed-race heritage, talking about his father, who had come to America from "one of the world's poorest nations," and his grandmother, who "worked on a bomber assembly line at Fort Leavenworth."

This narrative, as usual, was couched in terms that were "at once unique and universal, black and more than black." He sketched out a history of the union: the Founding Fathers had affirmed "equal citizenship under the law" while building their economy on the labor of slaves; since then the United States had failed to live up to its constitutional promise many times, but if it was to achieve its destiny—to wipe clean the "original sin of slavery"—its citizens would have to believe in the "improbable experiment" of a "more perfect union."

In other words, the path would be long and painful but waiting at the end of it was Obama himself:

> I am the son of a black man from Kenya and a white woman from Kansas . . . I have brothers, sisters, nieces, nephews, uncles, and cousins of every race and every hue, scattered across three continents, and for as long as I live, I will never forget that in no other country on Earth is my story even possible.

Though I'm the son of a yellow woman from Indonesia and a white man from Devon, with aunts, uncles, cousins, nieces, and nephews of many races and hues scattered across at least three continents, I couldn't see the connection between his words and my background.

What I heard wasn't a specific *I am* but an "infinite I AM." He was less a person than a crucible in which all manner of grievance and hurt had been melted down to forge a new, continent-spanning soul.

Obama's utopian language tapped into that of writers like the early-twentieth-century Mexican statesman and philosopher José Vasconcelos, who prophesied the coming of a *raza cósmica* (cosmic race) that would inherit the best qualities of every race. Vasconcelos called it "the matrix race of a new civilization."[105] Obama made clear this prophecy could only be fulfilled in America, the one "country on Earth" where his story was possible.

Perhaps this unblemished faith in America was all that could have overcome the white terror exposed by Wright's sermons. In making himself the superheroic, mixed creation of U.S. history's better side, Obama was no longer a threatening Other or a harbinger of racial mongrelization. He was manifest destiny itself.

Tony Blair had talked in anodyne fashion about a "new era of race relations," but Obama was—*e pluribus unum*—the superhuman embodiment of multiculturalism, containing within himself all races—black, white, yellow, and brown. Writing after the election in the *New Yorker*, Hendrik Hertzberg singled out this speech as central to his success: "In its combination of objectivity and empathy, it persuaded Americans of all colors that he understood them."[106]

I would put it another way: it succeeded in persuading Americans—mainly white—that they wouldn't need to wrap their minds around the complexities of history, its real and enduring hurts, because Obama's expanding consciousness would be large enough to wrap itself around them, to raise them all up together.

In *The Audacity of Hope,* Obama had set out the basis of this argument, reflecting on his famous speech at the 2004 Democratic Conference: "there's not a black America and white America and Latino America and Asian America—there's a United States of America." This "seemed to strike a chord," he wrote two years later. People wanted to be "freed from the past of Jim Crow and slavery, Japanese internment camps and Mexican braceros."[107]

Obama could skate over the different reasons that white people and people of color might have for wanting to escape the past because his argument was grounded in his own mixed-race experience: "In a sense I have no choice but to believe in this vision of America . . . I've never had the option of restricting my loyalties on the basis of race, or measuring my worth on the basis of tribe."[108]

He had no choice but to believe in an all-embracing, contradictory vision of America that reconciled everyone within him, because he loved both his black pastor—in spite of his fiery anti-American rhetoric—and his white grandma—in spite of her occasionally racist remarks. And voters, in placing their faith in Obama, could embrace that contradiction too, freeing themselves from the pain of conscious deliberation. This was in line with a Victorian vision—laid out by Carlyle and enunciated by Matthew Arnold, among others—of making "the State more and more the expression, as we say, of our best self, which is not manifold, and vulgar, and unstable, and contentious, and ever-varying, but one, and noble, and secure, and peaceful, and the same for all mankind."[109] Obama was the hero capable of expressing the State in himself, of lifting the past's tragic, contentious burden and so transcending it.

In the 1978 version of *Superman*, starring Christopher Reeves in the title role, Superman says, "I'm here to fight for truth and justice and the American way." He glorifies a certain kind of innocence which, though he's technically an alien, feels tied up with his wholesome middle-American upbringing. In Zack Snyder's *Man of Steel*, a general questions how he can know Superman won't "act against America's interests." "I grew up in Kansas," Superman replies. "I'm about as American as it gets." I think of how Nietzsche would have reacted to this half-alien and wholly Kansan *Übermensch*; he hated conventional notions of truth and justice and dismissed talk of a distinctively German "*folk* soul" as suffering from a "fatal vagueness."[110]

Keanu has more of a Nietzschean streak. Tentative and doubtful, he addresses the problem I had with the burly, all-American Superman—how can you be both innocent and indestructible?—by letting his vulnerabilities show. Like Nietzsche, his credo is *virescit volnere virtus*. Bernardo Bertolucci, who directed Keanu in *Little Buddha*, was asked about his casting and said Keanu had "an innocence I felt was crucial to the role of Siddhartha. His innocence is on his face and it goes to the core of his personality."[111]

In *Little Buddha*, Prince Siddhartha is in his early twenties when he begins to see beyond the dreamworld of the palace walls and decides, early one morning, to slip out and never return. Coming under the spell of a group of ascetic monks, he spends several years in the forest living off "a broth of mud or the droppings of a passing bird" until, one day, he hears music from a boat and sees a teacher scold his pupil: "If you tighten the string too much, it will snap. And if you leave it too slack, it won't play."

He realizes that *dukkha* (craving) can't be mastered through denial alone. Going to meditate between the gnarled roots of a fig tree, he resolves to find a Middle Way which, neither too tight nor too slack, will reconcile opposites.

Soon, though, the demon Mara hears word of Siddhartha and comes to tempt him. First he appears in the form of several beautiful women, who Siddhartha doesn't take much interest in. Then Siddhartha notices his reflection in the puddle in front of him begin to take on a more life-like form. He helps his puddle-doppelganger out of the water and they sit opposite one another, cross-legged.

"Architect, finally I have met you," Siddhartha says. "But I am your house and you live in me. O Lord of my own ego, you are pure illusion. You do not exist. The earth is my witness."

He touches the earth, covered in a potpourri of red and white blossom, and his mirror-self is revealed as none other than Mara—a short, stubbly man. Siddhartha smiles oddly, as if finally getting the punchline to a joke, a mandala of light buzzes around him, and he disappears. Having detached himself from himself and moved beyond illusion, he becomes Buddha, the Awakened One.

The Wachowskis must be alluding to this scene in *The Matrix Reloaded* when they have Neo meet a character—the creator and manifestation of the Matrix—called the Architect. A famously weird and confusing encounter (the word *ergo* is used a lot), in essence what's revealed is this: Neo, so far from being the One, is only the latest incarnation in a long line of Ones. What he has taken to be free will, the ego that has driven him this far, is pure illusion. He's the result of an "unbalanced equation," a recurring error in an otherwise smoothly functioning machine.

The suffusion of Buddhist ideas throughout the *Matrix* films makes their adoption by redpilling alt-righters particularly strange. As this scene shows, Neo is not a conventionally Superman-like character on a quest for self-knowledge; he isn't even a singular being—let alone a proponent of "truth, justice, and the American way"—but an "anomaly." The journey he goes on is toward self-diffusion, toward a realization that the earth exists; *you* do not.

In the words of Walter Kaufmann, the philosopher and Nietzsche scholar (whose translations were the first I read in an old Viking Portable Library edition), the *Übermensch* is someone who has undergone "a simultaneous preserving, cancelling, and lifting up."[112] Even in the name Nietzsche chose for his hero,

Über doesn't mean "super" in the sense of *amazing*, but something closer to "over" or "surpassing." I think it's Keanu's skill as an actor to communicate this sense of self-surpassing heroism—the hero both lifting up and negating himself—and, in his roles as Siddhartha and Neo especially, to create a charged vacancy, a space in which Self and Other can mix.

After leaving university I worked as a teaching assistant at a large state school in South West London. Like many people after university, thrown out into the world burdened with debt and no clear idea what to do, I felt lost.

One morning in January 2011, in the staff room before lessons, I read through the transcript of a speech Obama had given the night before. Shoes skidded past in the hallway outside. The previous week there had been an attempt to assassinate U.S. Congresswoman Gabrielle Giffords at a constituents' meeting in Tucson, Arizona. Giffords had been badly wounded and several others had been killed. Obama was leading the country in mourning.

He went through the names of the six who died—including Christina-Taylor Green, murdered before her tenth birthday—and those who tried to save others, like Patricia Maisch, the sixty-one-year-old woman who wrestled away the killer's ammunition. "Heroism is here, all around us," said Obama, "in the hearts of so many of our fellow citizens, just waiting to be summoned—as it was on Saturday morning."[113]

The political scientist George Blaustein has written about the power (and pitfalls) of Obama's oratory: "in the greatest Obama speeches, because of their eloquence and ceremonial grandeur, time itself slows. The *moment* is a sacred, baptismal pause ... The speech announces the moment, and it *is* the moment."[114]

It could have been because I was especially lost at the time—and surrounded by young children—but, reading that speech, I remember feeling held. Or, as Blaustein says, like time itself had slowed. And I don't think it's snide to say that the effect Obama generates in his best speeches—of momentous moment-ness—is movie-like. Not just in that they aspire to grandeur, but in that they actively draw their listeners into a variable timescape, one where the world might drop into slow motion—to draw out the full impact of a sentiment—or stop altogether.

In the movie *Hardball*, the character Keanu plays, Conor, gives a speech about a recently murdered student in which his phrases follow exactly the same elevated cadences as an Obama speech. Recounting the time he watched his student play baseball, Conor says: "I swear I was lifted in that moment to a better place. I swear he—he lifted the world in that moment. He made me a better person even if just for that moment."

I was lifted; he lifted the world; he made me a better person ...

The clauses almost seem to collapse in on themselves as Conor realizes it was "just for that moment." So long as it lasts, though, it defies gravity. For that moment—as in the moment of an Obama speech—no one is rich or poor, beautiful or ugly, native or alien, Self or Other. All are held and lifted and weightless.

That summer, in August 2011, a mixed-race man named Mark Duggan was shot dead by police officers in Tottenham Hale, North London. The police claimed that Duggan had shot first, but locals were skeptical. In the words of Martin Sylvester Brown, a member of a Haringey youth group, "Even if you didn't know him, you know nobody shoots at the police in Tottenham. You know, we've got, we've got a history."[115]

Stafford Scott, a civil rights campaigner in the community, said that a group of around fifty or so—among them Simone, the mother of Mark's children, along with friends and family from Mark's estate—marched to the police station. They carried simple banners, but didn't chant.[116] All they wanted was confirmation that Mark had actually been killed—information the police still hadn't provided. Instead, they were given the cold shoulder and told this was a matter for the Independent Police Complaints Commission.

Outside a crowd gathered—the BBC reported that three hundred people had joined in the march[117]—and a couple of kids started throwing vegetables at two parked police cars.

Though there were officers nearby, they kept their distance. More protesters arrived.

The estate in Tottenham that Mark lived on, Broadwater Farm, had been the site of intense rioting in 1985 after the deaths of Cynthia Jarrett and Cherry Groce—both after police raids. Tottenham, one of the most diverse areas of London, had remained one of the country's poorest since, with the highest rate of unemployment in London. Trust between police and the community was thin, and officers would later use this to justify their standoff as shops and vehicles burned.

The protests outside Tottenham Police Station soon spread across Haringey as the Carpetright building on the high road was set alight, police vehicles gasoline-bombed, and a retail park looted. The next evening, the riots spread to Enfield, Wood Green, and Dalston, neighboring areas with large black and minority ethnic populations disproportionately targeted by the police (in Dalston, July 2017, twenty-year-old Rashan Charles would die after being chased by police officers into a convenience store and pinned to the ground, prompting more protests).

By the third night, the rioting had spread to cities all over the country, from Bristol and Birmingham to Leeds and Liverpool, its motives now unconnected—at least directly—to Mark Duggan's shooting. Over the next two nights, ten thousand more police officers were deployed on British streets with orders to adopt a strict "zero-tolerance" approach, and the riots died down.

As they did, courtrooms across the country filled with offenders—mainly young, almost entirely male, and most likely not white—while politicians rushed to put their spin on what had happened.

A pause for some statistics: In 2010, a report by the Equality and Human Rights Commission showed that the proportion of black people in jail in the UK was almost seven times their share of the population—in the United States, by comparison, the proportion of black prisoners was four times greater than their population share. In 2017, according to government statistics, people of non-white ethnicities make up 26 percent of the prison population compared with 13 percent of the general population. In 2011, the police were 28 times more likely to stop and search black rather than white people. If you were black, you were also three times more likely to have a stun gun used against you. The "use of force" by police officers might also involve firearms, tear gas, and long-handed batons, along with physical restraint and restraint equipment. Data disclosed by the Metropolitan Police in August 2017 found that people of African descent and of ethnic minority background, in particular young African and Caribbean men, were twice as likely to die as white Britons after the use of force by police officers and the subsequent lack or insufficiency of access to appropriate healthcare.

According to the Race Disparity Audit in 2016, black and Asian households are twice as likely to be in persistent poverty as white households. Afro-Caribbean children are over three times more likely to be permanently excluded from school than white British pupils. E. Tendayi Achiume, the UN's Special Rapporteur on Human Rights, said in 2018 that "in some instances, schools refuse to implement appeal decisions calling for the readmission of wrongly excluded racial and ethnic minority children." The Equality and Human Rights Commission estimates that by the 2021/2022 tax year, the racially disparate impact of austerity measures adopted by the government between 2010 and 2017 will result in a 5 percent loss of income for black households, which is double the loss for white households. The Home Office reports that the number of hate crimes recorded by the police has more than doubled since 2012/2013, with 94,098 hate crime offenses recorded in 2017/18. The NatCen's British Social Attitudes Survey, running since 1983, shows that attitudes to sex outside of marriage, same sex marriage, and abortion have softened over the years, whereas the percentage of the population describing themselves as racially prejudiced, though it has varied slightly, has never fallen below 25 percent. Almost 70 percent describe themselves as "very or a little prejudiced."[118]

avid Cameron, then-Prime Minister, cut short his holiday in Tuscany to oversee the response to the riots—or, at least, to be seen responding—and on August 15 gave a speech at a youth center in his local constituency of Witney, Oxfordshire (where unemployment rates are among the lowest in the country at 1.5 percent).

"These riots were not about race," he said, nor were they about "government cuts" or "poverty." They were about "behaviour ... a twisted moral code." They happened because people no longer knew right from wrong, because Britain was "broken."[119]

His comments echoed those of his Education Secretary Michael Gove, who attributed the rioting to "a culture of greed and instant gratification, rootless hedonism and amoral violence."[120]

Cameron admitted, however, that "behaviour does not happen in a vacuum: it is affected by the rules government sets and how they are enforced." So these "twisted" riots, though they weren't about government cuts, were about "behaviour" which may have been affected by government rules. The government was and was not responsible.

There were countless other speeches by politicians, all keen to share their theories as to why it had happened (Michael Gove thought it could have been prevented if teachers were allowed to use "greater force" against their students and if young people joined their local cadets).[121]

Meanwhile almost two thousand people were being handed prison sentences, the majority for petty crimes—one twenty-three-year-old was given six months for stealing £3.50 worth of water.[122] According to statistics from the Ministry of Justice, 52 percent of those charged were black, Asian or "other"; 35 percent of adults involved were claiming out-of-work benefits at the time (the national average is 12 percent); and 42 percent of the young people involved were in receipt of free school meals (the national average is 16 percent).[123] But the riots were not about race or poverty, said the Prime Minister.

My own memories of that week are loose. I remember going to work, meeting friends, checking Twitter. I'd just moved out of Clapham Junction, where the rioting was briefly at its worst. I texted friends to ask how they were. A department store had been raided and a fancy dress shop set on fire. They said they were at home, checking Twitter too.

It had only been through someone's connection to a church-owned house with cheap rent that we'd ended up living in Clapham Junction, halfway between the railway station and Battersea. It felt like an in-between place in other ways too. Over the last couple of decades, Clapham had transformed itself into a popular residential area for bankers and young professionals, now known jokily as "Pram Springs" and full of cocktail bars and shops specializing in boutique baby wear.

Battersea, though, was still one of the most deprived parts of London. In 2013, the foodbank at St Mark's Church served 1,551 local people, two in five of whom were children. And if that proportion seems high, the Institute of Fiscal Studies predicts that by 2022 it will be the norm in Britain with child poverty reaching up to 37 percent.[124]

Maybe, as David Cameron said, this is a "broken" country, but the riots aren't what broke it. They exposed the fissures that were already there, which might once have been possible to see past. Beneath London's smoothly functioning surface, poverty had been on the rise, along with almost every indicator of racial disparity.

I struggle to relate Obama to the events of that summer. The heroism he summoned, the projected unity, the sharing in a single, clinched moment, feels dissonant. In Tucson, his words could lift the weight of tragedy. They could inspire. But they couldn't answer to the rage of protracted injustice. This much would become clear in Ferguson in 2014 when Obama was helpless to stem the tide of anger that followed the police shooting of Michael Brown. Sometimes no speech, however beautiful, can compensate for suffering.

In 2011, I was surprised. I hadn't expected the rage because I hadn't seen the injustice. Or I had shut my eyes to it—as I had to my own racial difference—half-looking away from the world in the hope that its troubles might disappear. In that case, I wouldn't have to bear responsibility for them. But the brokenness was everywhere around and inside of me.

ometimes I think that art needs to end in revelation: a previously unseen truth that shifts the world on its axis. This has its repercussions. If your aim is life-changing art, art must change your life. So you start to see your thoughts and relationships as though plotted on a graph, mapped against a series of epiphanic peaks and troughs. And if you don't reach those peaks—if you feel confused or like you're going nowhere—you've failed.

I have to remind myself that there isn't another reality that you can be redpilled—or redpill someone else—into seeing.

Think of the *Matrix* films. Directed by two transgender women, Lana and Lilly Wachowski, they're suffused with images of sexual and racial fluidity. Everyone wants to go to a party like that sweaty, underground rave in *The Matrix Reloaded*. Still, they've been taken up by alt-right fans who regard trans people as mentally ill.

Or think of when Dixon is deciding whether or not he should engage with that racist senator on his train. He would prefer not to—it will likely make no difference and could lose him his job—

but he remembers something. During a recent visit to the Bureau of Standards in Washington, he saw "the effect of the pressure of a single finger upon a supported bar of steel three inches thick. The slight strain had caused the steel to yield one-twenty-thousandth part of an inch, as the delicate apparatus, the interferometer, had registered."[125]

That slight strain, difficult to see, is harder to praise. But as Keanu once said, "the simple act of paying attention can take you a long way in life."[126] It's not what's being paid attention to that matters so much as the act of attention itself. How else do you change someone's mind? How does the most unforgiving matter yield? Not with a cathartic swoop or a piercing insight, but with the pressure of a single finger—or many fingers—held in place for a long time.

efore Thomas Carlyle, there was another kind of popular hero: the saint. Maybe the saint is better seen less in the context of the hero's or strongman's evolution than as running against it. While warrior-heroes strove against the gods, or could only please some while displeasing others, saints were granted whatever virtues they had as a result of their piety to those gods.

Thomas Aquinas believed that because God was a rational being he had endowed everyone with a purpose. For him, saints were humans with a particular skill for tuning into their purpose. This may not have allowed them to melt flesh with their eyes or combust at will, but it gave Abraham the superpower of faith, Moses meekness, and Job patience. Saints didn't have to be stronger or more magical than the rest of us; they had to be good at being themselves.

Virtues have a different quality to actions; they're not discrete. As Aquinas wrote, "good is diffusive of itself."[127] By this, I think he meant that moral goodness should only—maybe *can* only—be pursued for its own sake.

In the Sermon on the Mount, Jesus makes a similar point:

"when thou doest alms, let not thy left hand know what thy right hand doeth" (Matthew 6:3). If a "good" act is done to achieve a particular end, then the moral impulse will likely die with that deed. If you help someone carry their shopping to impress on-lookers—your left hand proudly watching over your right hand—you're less likely to do it again. But if "goodness" is not something you can succeed or fail at, being a state of diffusive virtue, it has no necessary end. It ripples into eternity.

This was the realization Obama claimed to have in *Dreams from My Father*. Working as a community organizer in Chicago, he observed how Harold Washington had towered over the city's politics, as a lawyer and then as its first black mayor. He was almost too singular and overwhelming a force: "the entire of black politics had centered on one man who radiated like a sun."[128] After he was gone, where did that leave his supporters and project?

Keanu's characters—the ones who understand this—are al-ways letting go, ceding control. In *Point Break*, Johnny Utah starts out in denial, trying to be someone he isn't—a soccer player, an FBI agent, a surfer—before choosing the path of self-diffusion. His mistake was ever thinking his identity needed to be fixed, that a hero has to look a certain way. At the end of the film—having let go of the criminal he's spent years chasing—Johnny throws his FBI badge into the sea. He discovers who he is by abandoning himself.

Toward the end of *Dreams from My Father*, Obama brushes his hand across the "smooth yellow tile" of his father's tomb. He wants to tell him that you can't become a "whole man" by leaving a part of yourself behind. He feels sated, though, no longer shut off from him. Meeting his Granny, he has a similar feeling: of a circle closing, being able to "recognize myself as I was, here, now, in one place."[129]

This way of putting it—in terms of self-recognition and completion—sets him apart from Keanu, whose characters usually couldn't care less about recognizing themselves, or about anyone recognizing them, least of all "here, now, in one place."

Where Keanu pauses, mumbles, and trails off, Obama is assured and steady. Life for him is the gradual piecing together of identity: black, white, American, Kenyan, Indonesian, Hawaiian; a native of Los Angeles, New York, and South Side, Chicago. These experiences, if properly understood, can be assembled to form a whole, a circle. Or, at least, it's his belief in this possibility which constitutes his heroism.

For Keanu, who wants to fit "all categories—and no categories," heroism is about dispersal. Far from being a "whole man," he celebrates his incompleteness and confusion. The various points of his identity are like stars, scattered and moving further apart.

In Hawaii, where Keanu's dad is from and where Obama went to high school, there are native Hawaiians, Chinese, Japanese, Filipinos, Samoans, Okinawans, and Portuguese, alongside white people from the mainland.

It's a microcosm of the world's variety—of a variety which is still growing. According to the Migration Observatory at the University of Oxford, there are more children of "mixed origins" than ever and more people choosing to identify their ancestry as "Other, mixed." Between 2001 and 2011, the number of "mixed" people in England and Wales grew by 82 percent.[130] Around the world, there are an endless variety of *pardos, ainoko, mestizos,* and *zambos.* Immigration and "intermarriage" aren't new phenomena; they're two of the few permanent facts about our shared history.

The mixed-race experience, if it means anything, isn't sad or lonely or heroic so much as *confusing.* Regardless of background, it should force us to consider the parts of ourselves we take for granted—ideas of race, nation, and wholeness—and to appreciate how our experience of the world is always mixed. That is, marked in equal parts by recognition and incomprehension.

Approaching his eightieth birthday, Goethe wrote a letter to Johann Peter Eckermann reflecting on his life: "Throughout the ages people have said again and again that one should try to know oneself. This is a strange demand with which nobody has complied so far, and with which nobody should comply."[131]

Man is a "dark being," Goethe wrote, "he does not know from where he comes nor where he goes; he knows little of the world, and least about himself."[132]

This was one point on which Goethe and Nietzsche agreed. In *Beyond Good and Evil*, Nietzsche writes about his "unconquerable mistrust of the *possibility* of self-knowledge." Though he could often seem scornful and self-assured, he felt that the "most certain thing" he could know about himself was this "aversion in me to *believing* anything definite about myself."[133]

This should give us hope. History doesn't have to be the story of brightly lit individuals, active and masculine, doing great deeds. Our stories don't have to be about achieving self-knowledge, or failing to do so. They can recognize the matrix of differences—along lines of class, race, gender, and sexuality—that shape our experience of the world. They can be about the spaces between.

Another letter, from Audre Lorde to the white feminist and academic Mary Daly in 1979, echoes this thinking: "When I speak of knowledge, as you know, I am speaking of that dark and true depth which understanding serves, waits upon, and makes accessible through language to ourselves and others. It is this depth within each of us that nurtures vision."[134] That "dark and true depth" of knowledge within us is capable of nurturing understanding precisely because it is unknown.

In *Little Buddha*, a class of young monks recite a sutra that could stand in for the lesson of all mixed-race supermen: "Form is empty. Emptiness is form. No eye, ear, nose, tongue, body, mind."

To be mixed-race is to exist in a state of paradox. Race is an illusion that depends on purity and singleness. The Mixed-Race Superman is paradox made manifest, emptiness as form.

In *A Scanner Darkly*, set in a paranoid surveillance state in the near-future, Keanu plays a government agent called Bob Arctor who, because he works undercover, has to wear a "scramble suit" in the office. This suit, projecting 1.5 million constantly shifting representations of different people—male and female, black, white, Latinx—keeps his identity cloaked. Even the people he works with have no idea who he is.

The scramble suit represents one of our oldest dreams: that of escaping the body. In the ancient world, octopuses were revered for their ability to change shape as they merged with their surroundings. The polytropic Odysseus, clinging onto a rock to avoid being carried off by the waves, is compared to an octopus.

And in a fragment by the lyric poet Theognis, written two centuries after Homer, the heart is as *tangled* and *complex* as an octopus, taking on the hue of its nearest rock. It's better, Theognis said, to have the craft and cunning of an octopus than to be *atropiis* (unchangeable).

In her 1997 biography of Keanu, Sheila Johnston recounts how "At the peak of his fame, Keanu made a sharp comment about himself and his admirers. 'I'm Mickey,' he said. 'They don't know who's inside the suit.' His friend retorted, 'But you're a movie star!' To which Keanu, laughing, replied, 'So's Mickey.'"[135] It's a nightmarish idea, being trapped in a Mickey suit and forced to wake up each day with a cartoon mouse's huge rictus grin. I wonder if Keanu, as an actor and person of color, is more sensitive to the idea—the horror—of being divided against yourself?

Race fixes what's apparent, transforming it into fate. Simone Weil's essay "*The Iliad*, or the Poem of Force" manages to write brilliantly about how this happens without mentioning race. Instead, she writes about force—"that *x* that turns anybody who is subjected to it into a *thing*"—using the world of the *Iliad* as her test case. There, the specter of death hangs over every character, whether terrified or hardened: "He is alive; he has a soul; and yet—he is a thing." And the force which elevates heroes like Achilles—allowing them to believe in their self-mastery—will inevitably bring them down, because "those who have force on loan from fate count on it too much and are destroyed." Force is "double-edged," writes Weil. It turns both the people who use it and those who endure it to stone.[136]

Maybe this is why, when asked where I was from in school, I'd hide behind my mixedness, spraying it like a jet of cloudy ink in the faces of those around me. It was a defense against power or force, against those who would fix me stone-like to a particular identity, so making me more *thing* than person. I wanted to be an octopus—shifting, complex, invisible at will.

Later, I came to think of this lack of stability as a fault. I should know myself, I said. But there's another vision of strength in the Classical world: of identity that survives difference and disguise. After all, what does Odysseus look like? When he needs to infiltrate Ithaca—as at other points in the epic—Athena alters his appearance. Form is empty. Emptiness is form. And if I try to picture him, to imagine his face, I see a hundred shifting features, all of them distinctly his own.

For people of color, the body is inescapable, and so is the power that others would have over it. This is why Obama's father sought to master power through force of intellect, and why Lolo fell silent.

Keanu's father, Sam, was another victim to power, unable or unwilling to escape his fate. After leaving behind his young family, Sam moved back to his birthplace of Hawaii and started dealing drugs, eventually getting arrested in 1994 carrying a bag of heroin and cocaine through Hilo International Airport. He publicly asked his son to intervene, but by this stage Keanu didn't want anything to do with him.[137]

In a *USA Today* interview from 1987, Keanu dismisses Sam as a "'60s deadhead reject."[138] But in a feature interview with Margy Rochlin from March 1995, published in *US Magazine*, he was more tender, talking about the last time he and his dad hung out properly when he was thirteen years old:

It was at night. We were in Kauai. And I remember him speaking about the stars. Something about how the world is a box.

And I looked up, and I had no clue what he was talking about. [Laughs] "No, Dad, the earth is round. It's not a rectangle, man." No, I'm sure he didn't say that. But I remember him speaking about the stars as we looked up.[139]

What links every "little outcast," says Langston Hughes, is a vision of America as "the star-seeking I."[140] Though I'm not American, I know that "star-seeking" impulse, that desire to be affirmed by a culture so certain of its destiny. The larger certainty of America pours into the individual "I."

The last time Obama saw his father—the only time, he says in his memoir, he can remember spending real time with him—he was nine. His memories are distorted by the few photographs that have survived. In one, they stand by a Christmas tree, Obama holding up a basketball that he's just been given, his father opaque, a "present mass."[141] It's funny, he says in one interview, that it was after this visit he started taking basketball seriously but for a long time he didn't connect the two events.

From one perspective, the past looks like a series of static images; from another, it looks like a flowing stream. Both perspectives are grounded in the same fear: that the past is really made of nothing at all; that the self that we hope to know and the narratives arising from that desire are pure illusion.

I picture the sky as a black tablecloth, stars spilt across it like grains of salt. I start to join the dots, looking for patterns, but Keanu and Obama—like Achilles and Odysseus—are nowhere to be seen.

However bright they glow, heroes emit an approximate light. The wonder we have in them stands in for our wonder in each other. For me, at least, this is the lesson of the Mixed-Race Superman: we are too few or too many, but never singular.

As I look at the stars, I give myself up to power. Though I no longer seek any particular form or shape, faces begin to emerge one by one—some of which I love a great deal—each without expression and endlessly expressive.

NOTES

1 Sheila Johnston, *Keanu Reeves* (London: Pan, 1997), 24.

2 Simone de Beauvoir, *The Second Sex* (trans. Constance Borde & Sheila Malovany-Chevallier; New York: Vintage Books, 2011), 26.

3 Donna Haraway, *Simians, Cyborgs, and Women: The Reinvention of Nature* (New York: Routledge, 1991), 177.

4 Vikram Dodd, "They treated me as a suspect—not a victim," *The Guardian* (25 February 1999): https://www.theguardian.com/uk/1999/feb/25/lawrence.ukcrime4.

5 Toni Morrison, "On the First Black President," *The New Yorker* (5 October 1998): https://www.newyorker.com/magazine/1998/10/05/comment-6543.

6 Quoted in David Gillborn, "Tony Blair and the Politics of Race in Education: Whiteness, Doublethink and New Labour," *Oxford Review of Education*, 34, no. 6 (December 2008): 714.

7 1997 Labour Party Manifesto, "New Labour Because Britain Deserves Better": http://www.labour-party.org.uk/manifestos/1997/1997-labour-manifesto.shtml.

8 Philip Johnston, "Adopt our values or stay away, says Blair," *The Daily Telegraph* (9 December 2006): https://www.telegraph.co.uk/news/uknews/1536408/Adopt-our-values-or-stay-away-says-Blair.html.

9 Dodd, "They treated me as a suspect – not a victim."

10 William MacPherson, The Stephen Lawrence Inquiry. Report of an Inquiry (1999): 51, https://www.gov.uk/government/publications/the-stephen-lawrence-inquiry.

11 David Remnick, *The Bridge: the Life and Rise of Barack Obama* (London: Picador, 2010), 82.

12 Remnick, *The Bridge*, 106.

13 Remnick, *The Bridge*.

14 Remnick, *The Bridge*, 201.

15 Friedrich Nietzsche, *Thus Spoke Zarathustra* (trans. Thomas Common; London: G. Allen and Unwin, 1932), 104.

16 Friedrich Nietzsche, *The Portable Nietzsche* (trans. Walter Kaufmann; Harmondsworth: Penguin, 1976), 127.

17 Nietzsche, *The Portable Nietzsche*, 139.

18 Elena Schneider, "Trump explains tweeting Mussolini quote" (2/28/2016): https://www.politico.com/story/2016/02/trump-tweets-interesting-mussolini-quote-219932.

19 Virgil, "The Age of the Lion: Donald Trump Puts America First": https://www.breitbart.com/politics/2017/01/20/virgil-age-lion-donald-trump-puts-america-first/.

20 Nietzsche, *The Portable Nietzsche*, 139.

21 Julian Symons, *Thomas Carlyle: The Life and Ideas of a Prophet* (London: Victor Gollancz, 1952), 165.

22 Fred Kaplan, *Thomas Carlyle: A Biography* (Ithaca, N.Y.: Cornell University Press, 1983), 265.

23 Thomas Carlyle, *On Heroes, Hero-Worship and the Heroic in History* (London: Chapman and Hall, 1840), 3.

24 Carlyle, *On Heroes* 25.

25 Carlyle, *On Heroes.*

26 Symons *The Life and Ideas of a Prophet*, 167.

27 Carlyle, *On Heroes*, 3.

28 Thomas Carlyle, "Occasional discourse on the Negro question," *Critical and Miscellaneous Essays in Five Volumes: Volume IV* (London: Chapman and Hall, 1869), 350.

29 Carlyle, "Occasional discourse on the Negro question," 376.

30 Carlyle, "Occasional discourse on the Negro question," 351.

31 Carlyle, "Occasional discourse on the Negro question," 374.

32 *The Epic of Gilgamesh* (trans. Andrew George; London, Penguin Books, 2003), 5.

33 Wyatt Mason, "The First Woman to Translate the 'Odyssey' Into English," *The New York Times Magazine*, February 11, 2017, https://www.nytimes.com/2017/11/02/magazine/the-first-woman-to-translate-the-odyssey-into-english.html.

34 Homer, *The Odyssey* (trans. Emily Wilson; New York: W.W. Norton and Company, 2018), 10.5.

35 Johnston, *Keanu Reeves* 168.

36 Chris Hardwick, "Keanu Reeves Returns," July 2, 2017, in The Nerdist Podcast #851, podcast, YouTube video, 2:00:31, https://www.youtube.com/watch?v=UL6IgZ9okss.

37 Hardwick, "Keanu Reeves Returns."

38 Perry Anderson, "Passing the Baton," *New Left Review* 103 (January–February 2017), 49.

39 See, for example, this from Obama's speech in Grant Park, Chicago, on November 11, 2008 after becoming the President-elect: "tonight, because of what we did on this date in this election at this defining moment change has come to America."

40 Anderson, "Passing the Baton," 50.

41 Dean Baquet, "Jay-Z & Dean Baquet," The New York Times Style Magazine, November 29, 2017, https://www.nytimes.com/interactive/2017/11/29/t-magazine/jay-z-dean-baquet-interview.html.

42 "Barack Obama at the Al Smith Dinner," RealClearPolitics, October 16, 1974, transcript, https://www.realclearpolitics.com/articles/2008/10/barack_obama_at_the_al_smith_d.html.

43 On Rush Limbaugh's characterization of Obama's "facial expressions" as "demonic": https://www.americanthinker.com/articles/2008/10/who_wrote_dreams_from_my_fathe_1.html; on images supposedly linking Obama to the Black Panthers: https://www.snopes.com/fact-check/obama-black-panther-photo/; on the claim that Bill Ayers was the ghost-writer of Dreams from My Father: https://www.americanthinker.com/articles/2008/10/who_wrote_dreams_from_my_fathe_1.html/.

44 From "Scottish Portraits" (1854), quoted in Michael K. Goldberg's introduction to Carlyle, On Heroes, xxxvi.

45 Quoted in A. R. Ammons, "A Poem Is a Walk" in Claims for Poetry, edited by Donald Hall (Ann Arbor: The University of Michigan Press, 1982), 1.

46 See, for example, James Cowles Prichard in 1843: "has man received from his Maker a principle of accommodation by which he becomes fitted to possess and occupy the whole earth? He modifies the agencies of the elements upon himself; but do not these agencies also modify him?," quoted in Michael Banton, Racial theories (Cambridge: Cambridge University Press, 1987), 23.

47 Thierry Hoquet, "Biologization of Race and Racialization of the Human: Bernier, Buffon, Linnaeus," in The Invention of Race: Scientific and Popular Representations, edited by Nicolas Bancel, Thomas David, and Dominic Thomas) New York: Routledge, 2014), 21.

48 Banton, Racial theories, 53

49 Count Joseph Arthur de Gobineau, "Recapitulation: The Respective Characteristics of the Three Great Races; The Superiority of the White Type, and, Within This Type, of the Aryan Family," in Jayne O. Ifekwunigwe, 'Mixed race' Studies: A Reader (London: Routledge, 2004), 40.

50 Hoquet, "Biologization of Race and Racialization of the Human," 25.

51 Hoquet, "Biologization of Race and Racialization of the Human," 26.

52 Charles Dickens, Martin Chuzzlewit (London: Penguin Books, 1986), 51.

53 Benjamin Disraeli, Coningsby; Or, The New Generation (Leipzig: Bernhard Tauchnitz, 1844), 204-05.

54 De Gobineau, "Recapitulation," 40.

55 Adolf Hitler, Mein Kampf (London: Hurst and Blackett, 1939), 231.

56 Barack Obama, Dreams from My Father: A Story of Race and Inheritance (Edinburgh: Canongate, 2008), 30.

57 Banton, Racial theories, 26.

58 Lothrop Stoddard, *Racial Realities in Europe* (New York: C. Scribner's Sons, 1925), 240–42.

59 Stoddard, *Racial Realities in Europe*, 246.

60 ForeverWhiteMan: https://www.stormfront.org/forum/t1168802/ (accessed February 12 2018).

61 Some examples: "impassive, inscrutable and just plain wooden" (*The Scotsman*, 16 June 2002): http://www.whoaisnotme.net/articles/2002_0616_why.htm; "Pondering the Mysterious Keanu Reeves" (Associated Press, November 5, 2003): http://www.whoaisnotme.net/articles/2003_1105_pon.htm; "the often-painfully laconic Reeves" (*Toronto Sun*, 14 September 2005): http://www.whoaisnotme.net/articles/2005_0914_ree.htm.

62 Leonard Klady, "Like a Chinese Menu," *Los Angeles Times*, (October 1, 1988): http://www.whoaisnotme.net/articles/1988_1001_lik.htm.

63 Remnick, *The Bridge*, 50.

64 R. L. Rutsky, "Being Keanu," in *The End of Cinema as We Know It*, edited by Jon Lewis (New York: NYU Press, 2001), 192.

65 Johnston, *Keanu Reeves* (London: Pan, 1997), 168.

66 Chris Heath, "The Pursuit of Excellence," *Details Magazine* (August 1991): http://www.whoaisnotme.net/articles/1991_08xx_pur.htm.

67 Louis de la Hamaide, "Keanu Reeves—What Is He Trying To Prove?" *Voici* (December 11-17, 1995): http://www.whoaisnotme.net/articles/1995_1211_kea.htm.

68 Michael Shnayerson, "The Wild One: Keanu Reeves on Sex, Hollywood and Life on the Run," *Vanity Fair* (August 1995): http://www.whoaisnotme.net/articles/1995_08xx_wil.htm.

69 Sara Ahmed, *Living a Feminist Life* (Durham: Duke University Press, 2017), 37.

70 Adrienne Rich, "Compulsory Heterosexuality and Lesbian Existence," *Signs*, Vol. 5, no. 4, in *Women: Sex and Sexuality* (Summer, 1980): 632.

71 Jean-Paul Chaillet, "Prince of Speed," *Premiere magazine* (September 1994): http://www.whoaisnotme.net/articles/1994_09xx_pri.htm.

72 http://proudboysusa.com/ (accessed December 18, 2018).

73 Nietzsche, *The Portable Nietzsche*, 124.

74 Audre Lorde, "Age, Race, Class and Sex," in *Your Silence Will Not Protect You* (UK: Silver Press, 2017), 94.

75 Quoted in Bertrand Russell, *History of Western Philosophy* (London: Routledge, 2005), 51.

76 Jim Turner, "Much Ado About Keanu," *Detour Magazine* (May 1993): http://www.whoaisnotme.net/articles/1993_05xx_muc.htm

77 Quoted in J. M. Coetzee, *White Writing: On the Culture of Letters in South Africa* (New Haven: Yale University Press, 1988), 12.

78 "New Era of Race Relations," BBC News online (February 24,1999): http://news
    .bbc.co.uk/1/hi/uk/285471.stm.

79 Michael Gove, "More than simply black and white," *The Times* (January 26, 1999).

80 Quoted in the documentary *Stephen: The Murder That Changed a Nation* (dir. James
    Rogan; first broadcast on BBC One, April 17, 2018).

81 Ibid.

82 Michael Gove, "Be politically astute, not politically correct," *The Times* (October 10,
    2000).

83 Gove, "Be politically astute, not politically correct."

84 See, for example, MSNBC's Chris Matthews: "He is post-racial by all appearances. You
    know, I forgot he was black tonight," https://www.realclearpolitics.com/video/2010/01
    /27/msnbcs_matthews_on_obama_i_forgot_he_was_black_tonight.html.

85 Carlyle, *On Heroes*, 19.

86 Deepak Chopra, "Obama and the Call: 'I Am America,'" *The Huffington Post* (Janu-
    ary 5, 2008): https://www.huffingtonpost.com/deepak-chopra/obama-and-the-call-i
    -am-a_b_80016.html.

87 Chopra, "Obama and the Call."

88 Deepak Chopra, *Seven Spiritual Laws of Superheroes* (London: Transworld, 2011),
    105.

89 Samuel Taylor Coleridge, *The Major Works* (Oxford: Oxford University Press,
    2008), 313.

90 Ralph Waldo Emerson, "Nature," in *The Essential Writings of Ralph Waldo Emer-
    son* (New York: Random House, 2000), 6.

91 J. A. Rogers, *From Superman to Man* (Chicago: The Goodspeed Press, 1917), 24.

92 Rogers, *From Superman to Man*, 128.

93 George Bernard Shaw, *Man and Superman: A Comedy and a Philosophy* (London:
    Penguin Books, 2000), 226.

94 Obama, *Dreams from My Father*, 11.

95 Obama, *Dreams from My Father*.

96 The Universal Declaration of Human Rights (proclaimed by the United Nations
    General Assembly in Paris on December 10, 1948): http://www.un.org/en/universal
    -declaration-human-rights/.

97 Remnick, *The Bridge*, 65.

98 Remnick, *The Bridge*, 62.

99 Remnick, *The Bridge*, 68.

100 Remnick, *The Bridge*, 59.

101 Obama, *Dreams from My Father*, 43.

102 Adrienne Rich, "Cartographies of Silence," in *The Dream of a Common Language:
     Poems 1974-1977* (New York: W. W. Norton & Co, 1978), 19.

103 Daniel Nasaw, "Controversial comments made by Rev Jeremiah Wright," *The Guardian* (March 18, 2008).

104 Alex Mooney and Peter Hamby, "Clinton: Wright would not have been my pastor," CNN, http://edition.cnn.com/2008/POLITICS/03/25/clinton.wright/.

105 José Vasconcelos, "The Cosmic Race," in *Modern Art in Africa, Asia and Latin America: An Introduction to Global Modernisms* (Oxford: Blackwell Publishing, 2013), 411.

106 Hendrik Hertzberg, "Obama Wins," *The New Yorker* (November 17, 2008).

107 Barack Obama, *The Audacity of Hope: Thoughts on Reclaiming the American Dream* (Edinburgh: Canongate Books, 2007), 231.

108 Obama, *The Audacity of Hope.*

109 Matthew Arnold, *Culture and Anarchy* (Oxford: Oxford University Press, 2006), 150.

110 Nietzsche, "Notes (1873)," in *Portable Nietzsche*, 41.

111 Kristine McKenna, "Keanu's Eccentric Adventure," *Los Angeles Times* (June 5, 1994): http://www.whoaisnotme.net/articles/1994_0605_kea.htm.

112 Walter Kaufmann, *Nietzsche: Philosopher, Psychologist, Antichrist* (Princeton: Princeton University Press, 1974), 236.

113 George Blaustein, "The Obama Speeches," *n+1* Issue 27: "Deep End" (Winter 2017): https://nplusonemag.com/issue-27/politics/the-obama-speeches/.

114 Quoted in Gillian Slovo, *The Riots* (London: Oberon Books, 2014), 858.

115 Slovo, *The Riots.*

116 "Barack Obama Tucson Speech in Full," *The Telegraph*, January 13, 2011, https://www.telegraph.co.uk/news/worldnews/us-politics/8256760/Barack-Obama-Tuson-Speech-in-full.html.

117 "Riots in Tottenham after Mark Duggan shooting protest," BBC News online (August 7, 2011).

118 List of sources quoted in this section: "Hate Crime, England and Wales, 2017/18: Statistical Bulletin," *Home Office* (October 16, 2018): https://assets.publishing.service.gov.uk/government/uploads/system/uploads/attachment_data/file/748598/hate-crime-1718-hosb2018.pdf; Nancy Kelley and Sarah Sharrock, "Racial prejudice in Britain today," *National Centre for Social Research* (September 2017): http://www.natcen.ac.uk/our-research/research/racial-prejudice-in-britain-today; Damien Gayle, "Structural racism at heart of British society, UN human rights panel says," *The Guardian* (April 27, 2018); E. Tendayi Achiume, "End of Mission Statement of the Special Rapporteur on Contemporary Forms of Racism, Racial Discrimination, Xenophobia and Related Intolerance at the Conclusion of Her Mission to the United Kingdom of Great Britain and Northern Ireland": https://www.ohchr.org/en/NewsEvents/Pages/DisplayNews.aspx?NewsID=23073&LangID=E (accessed January 18, 2019).

119 Allegra Stratton, "David Cameron on riots: broken society is top of my political agenda," *The Guardian* (August 15, 2011).

120 Matthew Barrett, "Michael Gove winds up public disorder debate and condemns 'a culture of greed and instant gratification, rootless hedonism and amoral violence,'" *Conservative Home* (August 13, 2011): https://www.conservativehome.com/left watch/2011/08/michael-gove-wrapping-up.html.

121 "Gove speech on 'the underclass' in full:" https://www.politics.co.uk/comment -analysis/2011/09/01/gove-speech-on-the-underclass-in-full (accessed February 9, 2018).

122 "Some England riot sentences 'too severe'," BBC News online (August 17, 2011): https://www.bbc.co.uk/news/uk-14553330.

123 Alan Travis and Simon Rogers, "Revealed: the full picture of sentences handed down to rioters," *The Guardian* (August 18, 2011).

124 Larry Elliott, "Child poverty in Britain set to soar to new record, says thinktank," *The Guardian* (November 2, 2017).

125 Rogers, *From Superman to Man*, 16.

126 Kristine McKenna, "Keanu's Eccentric Adventure."

127 Quoted in John F. Wippel, "Thomas Aquinas on the Ultimate Why Question: Why is There Anything at All Rather than Nothing Whatsoever," *The Ultimate Why Question: Why is There Anything at All Rather than Nothing Whatsoever*, edited by Wippel (Washington, D.C.: The Catholic University of America Press, 2013), 104.

128 Obama, *Dreams from My Father*, 288.

129 Obama, *Dreams from My Father*, 429.

130 David Coleman, "Immigration, Population and Ethnicity: The UK in International Perspective," The Migration Observatory at the University of Oxford (April 17, 2013): https://migrationobservatory.ox.ac.uk/resources/briefings/immigration-population -and-ethnicity-the-uk-in-international-perspective/ (accessed February 9, 2018).

131 Quoted in Johann Peter Eckermann, *The Question of Psychological Types: the Correspondence of C.G. Jung and Hans Schmid-Guisan, 1915-1916*, edited by John Beebe and Ernst Falzeder (Princeton: Princeton University Press, 2013), 67.

132 Eckermann, *The Question of Psychological Types*, 68.

133 Friedrich Nietzsche, *Beyond Good and Evil: Prelude to a Philosophy of the Future* (London: Penguin Books, 2003), 213.

134 Audre Lorde, "Letter to Mary Daly," *Your Silence Will Not Protect You* (UK: Silver Press, 2017), 40.

135 Johnston, *Keanu Reeves*, 6.

136 Simone Weil, "The *Iliad* or the Poem of Force," in *Simone Weil: An Anthology* (London: Penguin Books, 2005), 183-204.

137 Reg Fitz and Dani Cestaro, "'Speed' Star's Nightmare As Dad Is Jailed In Cocaine Bust," *The National Inquirer* (July 12, 1994): http://www.whoaisnotme.net/articles /1994_0712_spe2.htm.

138 Quoted in Tom Green, "Keanu's Artistic Adventures," *USA Today* (18 July 1991): http://www.whoaisnotme.net/articles/1991_0718_kea.htm.

139 Margy Rochlin, "Keanu Reeves: The US Interview," *US Magazine* (March 1995): http://www.whoaisnotme.net/articles/1995_03xx_kea.htm.

140 Langston Hughes, "Star Seeker," in *The Collected Poems of Langston Hughes* (New York: Vintage Books, 1995), 64.

141 Obama, *Dreams from My Father*, 70.

ACKNOWLEDGMENTS

Like any work of criticism, this essay would have been impossible without the love and labor of many others. A special mention should go to the selfless scholarship of the Keanuphile(s) behind whoaisnotme.net. This essay was begun in August 2017, written and revised in London and Jakarta, and published in an earlier version in the UK in May 2018. It wouldn't have happened without Sam, Jake, and Will at Peninsula Press. Thank you to them, and to Dennis, whose insights made this new and enlarged version possible. Thanks always to my parents and to every part of my mixed family, including the Farrs and Aisha especially. This essay is for them and for anyone else who, like me, feels perpetually confused.

ABOUT THE AUTHOR

Will Harris is a London-based poet and critic. He is the author of the chapbook of poems, *All this is implied*, and was the recipient of the Arts Foundation's 2019 Poetry Fellowship. His work has appeared in *The Guardian*, the *London Review of Books*, and elsewhere. His first full poetry collection, *RENDANG*, is forthcoming from Granta in 2020.